SCIENCE
FOUNDATIONS

Kingdoms of Life

SCIENCE FOUNDATIONS

The Big Bang
Cell Theory
Electricity and Magnetism
Evolution
The Expanding Universe
The Genetic Code
Germ Theory
Gravity
Heredity
Kingdoms of Life
Light and Sound
Matter and Energy
Natural Selection
Planetary Motion
Plate Tectonics
Quantum Theory
Radioactivity
Vaccines

SCIENCE
FOUNDATIONS

Kingdoms of Life

PHILL JONES

CHELSEA HOUSE
An Infobase Learning Company

Science Foundations: Kingdoms of Life

Copyright © 2011 by Infobase Learning

Chelsea House
An imprint of Infobase Learning
132 West 31st Street
New York, NY 10001

Library of Congress Cataloging-in-Publication Data
Jones, Phill, 1953–
   Kingdoms of life / by Phill Jones.
      p. cm. — (Science foundations)
   Includes bibliographical references and index.
   ISBN 978-1-60413-340-0 (hardcover)
   1.   Biology—Juvenile literature. 2.   Life (Biology)—Juvenile literature.
3. Biology—Classification—Juvenile literature. I. Title. II. Series.

   QH309.2.J66 2011
   570—dc22   2010030581

Chelsea House books are available at special discounts when purchased in bulk quantities for businesses, associations, institutions, or sales promotions. Please call our Special Sales Department in New York at (212) 967-8800 or (800) 322-8755.

You can find Chelsea House on the World Wide Web at
http://www.chelseahouse.com

Text design by Kerry Casey
Cover design by Alicia Post
Composition by EJB Publishing Services
Cover printed by Yurchak Printing, Landisvile, Pa.
Book printed and bound by Yurchak Printing, Landisvile, Pa.
Date printed: April 2011
Printed in the United States of America

10 9 8 7 6 5 4 3 2 1

This book is printed on acid-free paper.

All links and Web addresses were checked and verified to be correct at the time of publication. Because of the dynamic nature of the Web, some addresses and links may have changed since publication and may no longer be valid.

Contents

Classifying Life on Earth

E arth teems with life. Scientists estimate that the planet may support 30 million different types of organisms. So far, less than 2 million have been discovered and classified. Humans tend to classify living things. Assigning animals to groups helped ancient hunters decide if they faced prey or predator. Early farmers selected certain plants to grow as a source of food. For several thousand years, humans have devised various schemes to classify living things. The challenge of classification is to find important traits that distinguish one animal from another. Consider a snake and a lamprey. They both have eel-like shapes and can be found in water. However, a snake has a jaw, whereas a lamprey is jawless. A snake breathes with lungs; a lamprey has gills. Which of these traits define a lamprey and a snake? Attempts to devise a formal scheme of classification continue to this day.

CLASSIFYING WITH HIERARCHIES

Historians credit Aristotle as the inventor of the first classification system of living things. Born in northern Greece in 384 B.C., Aristotle received training in medicine and taught himself about the structure of various animals. Around 350 B.C., Aristotle produced a series of

Figure 1.1 A lamprey is a jawless fish with a tooth-surrounded, funnel-like sucking mouth. Lampreys resemble eels because they have no scales, but they have seven gill pores on each side of their head.

10 books entitled *History of Animals,* in which he proposed a way to classify life into a hierarchical order. A hierarchical order is a ranked order. Hierarchies are very common. People use them every day. A book's table of contents displays the hierarchy of a book, for example. In the early days of the World Wide Web, people found information by drilling down from the top level of a directory to the lowest level. One of the most famous of the Internet guides was called "Yet Another Hierarchical Officious Oracle," or YAHOO!

Aristotle pictured his hierarchical scheme as a "ladder of nature" from the simplest life form to the most complex. Lifeless matter occupied the lowest rung of the ladder, followed by simple plants, complex plants, and on up to the top rung held by humans. To classify plants and animals, he picked certain traits and then grouped life forms with similar characteristics. For example, the first trait that he used to divide all life forms was the presence or absence of red blood. Life forms with red blood included humans, birds, reptiles, amphibians, fishes, and whales. Groups that lacked red blood included squids, octopuses, insects, jellyfish, and sponges. Within these two groups, he then divided those animals that bear live young and those that produce eggs. He continued to group animals by similar traits. Years later, Theophrastus, Aristotle's student, divided plants according to general form: herbs, shrubs, and trees.

Animals That Classify

Humans classify elephants, and elephants classify people. In Kenya, elephants are familiar with young Maasai men who spear elephants and the farming Kamba men who pose little threat to elephants. Researchers tested Kenyan elephants' ability to classify humans by presenting the animals with clean clothing and with clothing worn for five days by a Maasai or a Kamba man. Of the three types of clothing, the garments worn by the Maasai provoked the greatest fear in the animals. Then, the researchers showed the elephants samples of clean, red cloth and clean, white cloth. The sight of red clothing also disturbed the elephants, perhaps because young Maasai men often wear red clothing. The studies indicate that elephants use scent and clothing color to classify humans into groups that pose different risks to them.

Bats are another type of animal that classifies life forms. They do not use scent or color to classify; bats detect traits with sound. As they soar through the night air, the animals emit high-pitched sounds and receive returning echoes with ears that have a complex assortment of folds. Bats interpret echoes to determine distance, movement, and size of objects in their path. They also classify plants with their echoes. The animals use plants not only as food sources, but also as navigation markers to find favorite areas that contain food and to locate the path home. Plant echoes are very complex; many reflections from leaves and branches combine to produce the signal. Scientists are using computer models to understand how bats interpret plant echoes to classify plants.

For about 2,000 years, scientists continued to use the ancient Greek classification system with various tweaks. In 1694, French botanist Joseph Pitton de Tournefort published *Elements of Botany*, in which he classified plants according to their size and flower structure. The botanist assigned each type of plant a **species** name and grouped similar species into a genus.

Swedish naturalist Carl Linnaeus studied *Elements of Botany*. In 1735, he published his own book, an 11-page pamphlet entitled *System of Nature*. Linnaeus divided nature into three kingdoms: plant, animal, and mineral. After a while, he eliminated minerals from this classification scheme and focused on plants and animals. By the time he published the twelfth edition in 1770, his book had expanded to three volumes and more than 3,000 pages.

Linnaeus assigned a unique name, a species name, to each plant and animal and grouped similar species into genera (the plural of genus). He then grouped similar genera into orders, similar orders into classes, and continued grouping into ranks until he reached the highest level, the kingdom. Scientists still use Linnaeus's hierarchal system, although the ranks of animals now include kingdom, phylum, class, order, family, genus, and species, as well as various subgroups. As an example, dogs may be classified with nine levels of ranks:

> **Kingdom:** Animalia
> **Phylum:** Chordata
> **Subphylum:** Vertebrata
> **Class:** Mammalia
> **Order:** Carnivore
> **Suborder:** Caniformia
> **Family:** Canidae
> **Genus:** *Canis*
> **Species:** *familiaris*

This is just one way that scientists classify dogs. Some scientists consider domestic dogs to be a subspecies of the gray wolf. In this scheme, a dog is not *Canis familiaris*, but *Canis lupus familiaris*.

The two-kingdom system of Linnaeus grew during the nineteenth century. German scientist Karl Theodor Ernst von Siebold examined one-celled organisms with his microscope. In 1845, he published a book about protozoa, one-celled life forms that move

Figure 1.2 Carl Linnaeus devised a hierarchical system for classifying living things.

and search for food. He suggested that protozoa should be included in the animal kingdom. Other scientists disagreed, arguing that protozoa belong in the plant kingdom. In 1866, German biologist Ernst

Haeckel asserted that protozoa are neither plants nor animals. He placed them in their own kingdom.

As microscopes continued to improve, scientists realized that a three-kingdom system was too simple. During the 1930s, French marine biologist Edouard Chatton studied strange members of the protozoan group that lacked a structure in their cells called a **nucleus**. Chatton suggested that all life forms should be divided into two groups: cells that lack a nucleus (**prokaryotes**) and cells that contain a nucleus (**eukaryotes**). The eukaryote group would include both single-cell life forms that have a nucleus as well as multicellular life forms composed of cells with nuclei. Soon, there were four kingdoms: bacteria, protozoa (the protists), plants, and animals. The kingdom of bacteria contained prokaryote cells.

During the 1950s, American scientist Robert Whittaker argued that fungi and plants should not share a single kingdom. Fungi had been classified as plants, partly because fungi and plants do not move to hunt food. As an ecologist, Whittaker realized that plants and fungi differ in an essential way. Plants produce their own nutrients whereas fungi obtain nutrients by decomposing plant and animal matter. He proposed a fifth kingdom for fungi.

Classification of a life form in the five kingdom system focused on body and cell anatomy, features of reproduction, methods for obtaining food, and other observable traits. American scientist Carl Woese and German scientist Ralph Wolfe devised a new way to classify life forms. They studied the chemical structure of ribosomal **ribonucleic acid (RNA)** molecules of bacteria. Cells use ribosomal RNA, or rRNA, to make proteins, which are molecules that carry out many functions required to sustain life. An rRNA molecule consists of a chain of nucleotides, and each nucleotide contains a molecule called a **base**. RNA molecules have four types of bases: adenine, cytosine, guanine, and uracil. Woese and Wolfe discovered that bacteria can be divided into two groups due to differences in the structure of rRNA molecules and the sequence of their nucleotide bases: the eubacteria ("true bacteria") and the archaebacteria ("ancient bacteria"). The archaebacteria include bacteria that thrive in extreme **habitats,** such as acid lakes, hot springs, or water containing high concentrations of salt. In 1977, Woese proposed a sixth kingdom for the archaebacteria: the archaea.

CLASSIFYING WITH TREES

While some scientists improved hierarchical schemes, others worked on a different way to classify living things. The new method began with a long ocean voyage of a seasick amateur scientist.

In December 1831, 22-year-old Charles Darwin settled into a room aboard the brig HMS *Beagle*. Captain Robert FitzRoy, who was only four years older than Darwin, had wanted a man on board with an interest in science to join his survey mission. Darwin fit the description. Although he had shown a lack of interest in studies of classical literature, medicine, and religion, Darwin had always been fascinated with nature. Darwin and two survey officers shared a cramped room at the stern of the *Beagle* that contained a bookshelf, oven, cabinets, a wash stand, and a large chart table. The young scientist slept in a hammock suspended over the chart table, just below the ceiling. Every night, before climbing into his hammock, Darwin removed a drawer from a wall to make room for his feet.

The HMS *Beagle* set sail under clear skies from Plymouth, England. Darwin became seasick, a malady that plagued him for the next five years. Despite his illness, Darwin found his trip around the world invaluable. "The voyage of the *Beagle* has been by far the most important event in my life, and has determined my whole career," Darwin wrote in his autobiography. "I have always felt that I owe to the voyage the first real training or education of my mind."

Darwin only spent a combined 18 months at sea during his five-year journey. He explored on land most of the time. His observations of new plants and animals, as well as discoveries of fossils, led him to a revolutionary idea. He decided that plant and animal species changed over time. This contradicted a popular notion that living things had remained unchanged since the dawn of creation. When he began to work on his theory of evolution, Darwin drew a crude tree with ancient life forms at the bottom and descendants branching off along the trunk. Contrary to common belief, his evolutionary tree showed that different species are related to each other, and that organisms alter traits as they evolve.

After Darwin introduced the idea that living things evolve, some scientists decided that it was not enough to classify species in a fixed hierarchical system. Instead, classification should show possible

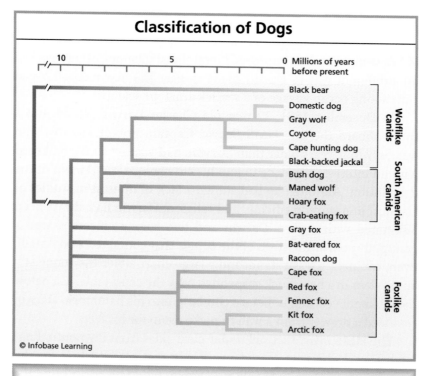

Classification of Dogs

Figure 1.3   This tree showing the evolution of dogs (family *Canidae*) was developed by Professor Robert Wayne and his colleagues at the University of California. Doing so required a variety of techniques, including the evaluation of skulls, skeletons, and chromosomes, as well as analysis of mitochondrial DNA, nuclear DNA, and proteins.

evolutionary relationships of life forms within a kingdom and between kingdoms. A branching diagram called a phylogenetic tree shows these potential relationships. A phylogenetic tree resembles Darwin's evolutionary tree in which the root of the tree represents ancestral lineage. Descendants of the ancestor are placed at the tips of branches.

In 1990, microbiologist and physicist Carl R. Woese proposed one popular phylogenetic tree called the three-domain system. Analyses of rRNA and chemical analyses of cells had shown that plants, fungi, animals, and single-celled protists have more in common with one another than archaea have in common with bacteria. Woese proposed that all life forms should be divided into an archaea domain, a bacteria domain, and a eukarya domain. The eukarya

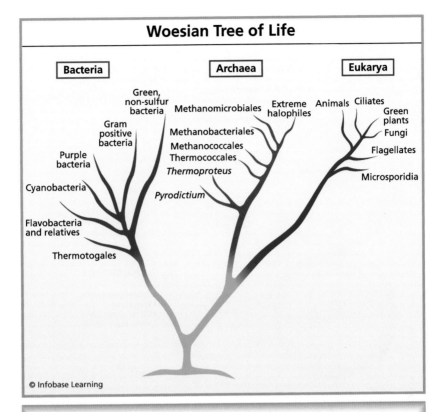

Woesian Tree of Life

Bacteria

Archaea

Eukarya

Green, non-sulfur bacteria

Methanomicrobiales

Extreme halophiles

Animals

Ciliates

Green plants

Gram positive bacteria

Methanobacteriales

Fungi

Methanococcales

Flagellates

Purple bacteria

Thermococcales

Thermoproteus

Cyanobacteria

Microsporidia

Pyrodictium

Flavobacteria and relatives

Thermotogales

© Infobase Learning

Figure 1.4 Professor Carl R. Woese defined a new kingdom of life, called Archaea, in 1977. He also redrew the taxonomic tree to make it a three-domain system. He based it on genetic relationships rather than morphological similarities, and divided life into 23 main divisions incorporated within three domains.

domain includes divisions for plants, protists, fungi, and animals. A hypothetical ancestor sits at the root of the three-domain tree. From this root, one branch gives rise to the bacteria, while a second branch gives rise to the archaea and eukarya.

MODERN CLASSIFICATION SCHEMES

Aristotle classified organisms by their general shape and internal anatomy. Over time, scientists selected traits based on cell structure and then the composition of molecules. Scientists disagreed over

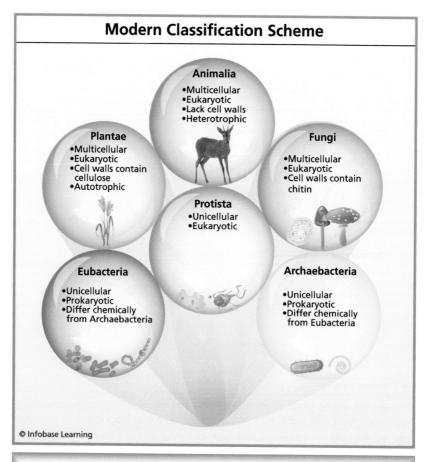

Modern Classification Scheme

Animalia
- Multicellular
- Eukaryotic
- Lack cell walls
- Heterotrophic

Plantae
- Multicellular
- Eukaryotic
- Cell walls contain cellulose
- Autotrophic

Fungi
- Multicellular
- Eukaryotic
- Cell walls contain chitin

Protista
- Unicellular
- Eukaryotic

Eubacteria
- Unicellular
- Prokaryotic
- Differ chemically from Archaebacteria

Archaebacteria
- Unicellular
- Prokaryotic
- Differ chemically from Eubacteria

© Infobase Learning

Figure 1.5 The six kingdom classification scheme became necessary after use of the modern microscope led to the discovery of new organisms and the identification of differences in cells.

the philosophy of classification. Some preferred a phylogenetic approach, while others remained faithful to traditional hierarchical systems. The disputes over classification continue. Today, the three-domain classification system is one popular phylogenetic system. Yet even among those scientists who prefer the phylogenetic approach, some argue that the classic evolutionary tree should be abandoned. A simple tree does not reflect complex evolutionary relationships, they say. Other scientists still use a kingdom-based hierarchical system.

Ant from Mars

Graduate student Christian Rabeling labored in a Brazilian rain forest to complete work for his master's thesis. He was mapping entrances to ant nests when he spotted a weird-looking ant. The insect had a pale body, large pincer-like mouth parts, and lacked eyes. This bizarre blend of traits inspired the name *Martialis heureka*; *Martialis* means "of Mars." The underground-dwelling ant has been assigned to the first new subfamily of living ants discovered in more than 85 years.

Rabeling and his associates examined details of the ant's anatomy and analyzed its **deoxyribonucleic acid (DNA)**, which encodes the creature's proteins. Their studies indicate that the ant is a descendant of one of the first types of ants to appear more than 120 million years ago. At that time, ants were just evolving from wasp ancestors. Rabeling suggests that wasp-like ancestors of *Martialis heureka* adapted to life underground, losing their eyes and gaining their pale body color.

The following chapters focus on the six-kingdom system with the kingdoms of eubacteria, archaea, protists, fungi, plants, and animals. We will explore the types of life forms that make up the kingdoms, organisms such as bacteria that thrive in ocean floor thermal vents, one-celled protozoans that shoot prey using darts tipped with a paralyzing toxin, a fungus that weighs hundreds of tons, and an animal that eats by turning its stomach inside out and pushing it out of its mouth and onto food.

Bacteria and Archaea

Bacteria are the smallest living things on Earth. The largest—the Moby Dick of the bacteria world—has a length of 0.02 inch (500 microns). Most bacteria are 500 times, or even billions of times, smaller. For more than a thousand years, scientists proposed the existence of life forms too small to be seen by the human eye. Proof that these tiny living things inhabit the world awaited the invention of the microscope.

Antonie van Leeuwenhoek, a seventeenth-century Dutch textile merchant, offered the first evidence that bacteria exist. In the textile trade, merchants examined the quality of goods using magnifying glasses to count thread densities. The practice might have inspired van Leeuwenhoek to explore the world hidden just beyond his eyesight. He built a simple microscope. One day, he focused his microscope on a mixture of clean rainwater and a white, gummy matter that he had scraped from his teeth. Van Leeuwenhoek reported that the mix contained "many very small living animals, which moved very prettily." He called the tiny creatures animalcules.

As scientists improved magnifying instruments, they discovered more details about microscopic organisms (microbes). In 1875, German biologist Ferdinand J. Cohn proposed an early scheme for classifying bacteria based on whether a microbe had a shape like a sphere, rod, fiber, or screw. Fifty years later, French marine biologist Edouard Chatton studied bacteria and other small organisms with improved microscopes. He proposed that life on Earth can be

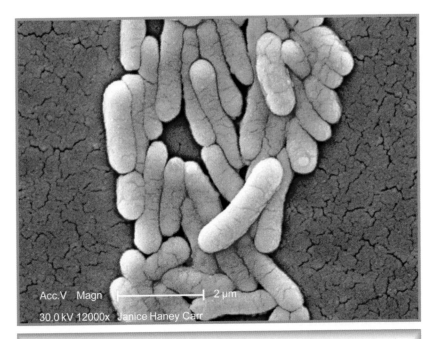

Acc.V Magn ⊢————————⊣ 2 µm
30.0 kV 12000x Janice Haney Carr

Figure 2.1   Under a high magnification of 12,000x, this colorized scanning electron micrograph revealed the presence of clustered Gram-negative salmonella bacteria.

divided into two groups based upon the presence or absence of a nucleus within a cell. Bacteria, which lack a nucleus, are prokaryotes. Life forms that have a nucleus in their cells are eukaryotes.

Today, scientists further divide the group of prokaryotes into two kingdoms: the eubacteria ("true bacteria") and the archaea ("ancient"). The eubacteria, or simply "bacteria," are the microbes studied by van Leeuwenhoek, Cohn, Chatton, and many others. They are the classic bacteria. The archaea are a newly discovered group of microbes often found thriving in harsh environments. One major difference between the groups is that archaea do not infect humans, whereas bacteria can inflict lethal diseases.

Studies of fossils indicate that prokaryotes have thrived on the planet for more than 3 billion years. Today, Earth's prokaryotes may total about 5 nonillion, or 5×10^{30}. Earth's prokaryotes may be a billion times more plentiful than the number of stars in the universe.

Due to their vast numbers, prokaryotes profoundly affect other life forms. Prokaryotes add oxygen to the air. As they degrade dead plant and animal tissues, prokaryotes release carbon dioxide and other inorganic molecules into the environment. Soil-dwelling prokaryotes remove carbon and other atoms from inorganic sources and use them to produce organic materials that enrich the soil for plant growth. The many forms of life on Earth could not exist without the little prokaryotes.

THE PROKARYOTE CELL

Prokaryotes are one-celled organisms that do not develop into multicellular forms. It is true that prokaryotes can grow as masses of cells. However, cells within a mass do not work together, as do cells in a plant or animal tissue. One prokaryote cell does not rely upon another prokaryote cell for survival.

A prokaryote cell can be divided into two parts: the **cytoplasm** and a cell envelope. The cytoplasm is a gel-like matrix that fills the interior of the cell. It is in the cytoplasm that the chemical reactions needed for life take place. The cytoplasm contains three types of molecules that play vital roles in maintaining the life of a cell: proteins, deoxyribonucleic acid (DNA), and ribonucleic acid (RNA).

- **Proteins:** Proteins are the cell's workhorses. Certain proteins maintain the cell's structure. Other proteins break down molecules for energy and build molecules needed for the cell to survive.
- **DNA:** Most prokaryotes have a single molecule of DNA, which contains the genetic information needed to produce proteins. On Earth, most living things synthesize proteins using the same genetic code to translate DNA's instructions. Prokaryotes reproduce by binary fission in which one cell divides into two cells that are usually identical to the original cell. Before binary fission, a cell synthesizes a copy of its DNA molecule. After cell division, each of the two cells contains a DNA molecule with the same information for producing proteins.
- **RNA:** RNA molecules play a vital role in the synthesis of proteins. Certain RNA molecules convey genetic

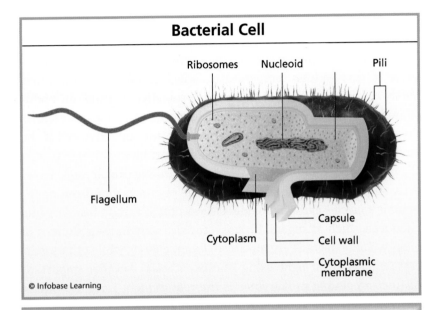

Bacterial Cell

Ribosomes   Nucleoid   Pili

Flagellum

Capsule

Cytoplasm   Cell wall

Cytoplasmic
membrane

© Infobase Learning

Figure 2.2   Bacteria are prokaryotes, lacking well-defined nuclei and membrane-bound organelles and having chromosomes composed of a single closed DNA circle.

information from DNA to the cell's protein synthesis machinery. A bacterial cell synthesizes proteins at structures called ribosomes, which contain proteins and RNA.

Most prokaryotes have a cell envelope that consists of at least two parts: a **plasma membrane** and a cell wall. The plasma membrane encloses the cytoplasm and controls the types of molecules entering and leaving a cell. A rigid cell wall encloses the plasma membrane and imparts a shape to the cell. The wall also prevents a cell from bursting like an over-filled water balloon when water flows into the cytoplasm. Certain species have a capsule, a coating of complex sugars that covers the cell wall. A capsule can prevent a single-celled predator from consuming the prokaryote cell. Some prokaryotes that live in soil have a capsule that prevents the cell from drying.

Depending on the species, a prokaryote cell may have appendages attached to the outside of the cell wall. Flagella are hair-like structures that move like propellers. Cells use flagella to swim toward nutrients and away from danger. Some species have another type of hair-like structure called pili. Pili enable a cell to attach to a surface, such as a rock or a tooth.

A number of prokaryotes form an inactive cell called an endospore to survive high temperatures, a lack of nutrients, and other harsh conditions. With their tough, protective coating, an endospore may be the sturdiest cell found in nature. An endospore shows no sign of life. Yet, it can transform back into an active cell if the environment changes to one that can support life.

Nutritional requirements vary widely among prokaryotes. However, all prokaryotes need carbon. Some obtain carbon from an inorganic source—carbon dioxide. Others obtain carbon from organic chemicals, such as sugars. Prokaryotes also vary in their sources of energy. Some degrade chemicals to obtain energy, while others generate energy from light using photosynthesis. Another important distinction among prokaryotes is the requirement for atmospheric oxygen. Cells that are obligate aerobes can grow only in the presence of oxygen. Obligate anaerobes can grow only in the absence of oxygen. For them, oxygen is a poison that interferes with cellular processes. Still other prokaryotes are flexible about the presence of oxygen. They switch metabolic processes depending upon the presence or absence of oxygen.

Over the billions of years that prokaryotes have lived on our planet, they have adapted to most environments. Some prokaryotes thrive in near-freezing Arctic waters, and others make their home in near-boiling water of hot springs. Some live on mountaintops, and some dwell on the ocean floor. Prokaryotes also live inside other life forms.

KINGDOM EUBACTERIA: CLASSIC BACTERIA

Bacteria can be classified in many ways. For example, bacteria can be divided into groups on the basis of their reaction to oxygen. Do the bacteria need oxygen to survive? Perhaps the bacteria do not need oxygen but they can tolerate it. Or, is oxygen lethal for them? Scientists can group bacteria based on their source of carbon: carbon dioxide or organic chemicals. Bacteria can be classified by physical traits, such as cell shape, presence of appendages (pili or flagella), ability to form endospores, and the presence of certain chemicals in the cell wall. Until recently, scientists had classified bacteria by their metabolic and physical traits. That changed with the invention of methods for analyzing RNA and DNA molecules.

A **gene** can be pictured as a piece of a DNA molecule that contains coded instructions for synthesizing a protein or an RNA molecule. In a modern classification system, bacteria are grouped by the composition of a gene encoding an RNA molecule that binds with ribosomes. This is the 16S ribosomal RNA gene, or 16S rRNA gene. The 16S rRNA gene has existed for at least millions of years. As species evolved, the gene altered slightly, so that different species have distinct 16S rRNA genes. By comparing differences in the rRNA gene and the rRNA molecule of different organisms, scientists could distinguish one species from another. Analysis of 16S rRNA also revealed that prokaryotes can be divided into the eubacteria (bacteria) and the archaea. Physically, these two types of prokaryotes appear similar. But, they differ in 16S rRNA, and in the composition of cell walls and cell membranes. Achaea also have genes that bacterial cells lack.

Most bacteria may live in subsurface layers of the land and oceans. However, many dwell within plants and animals, which rely upon the metabolic activities of the tiny cells for survival. As an example, certain bacteria live in the roots of pea plants and use nitrogen from the atmosphere to produce nitrogen-containing organic compounds required by the plants. Cows also depend upon prokaryotes. The stomach of a cow is divided into four compartments. The largest compartment is home to billions of bacteria that digest cellulose in grass and produce nutrients for the cow. In these two examples, the bacteria and their host enjoy a symbiotic relationship—that is, the association is mutually beneficial for the bacteria and the host. Bacteria also form parasitic relationships, in which the host may suffer injury and die.

The human body provides a home for many bacteria. An adult human carries a population of bacteria that weighs about a quarter of a pound (about 100 grams). The majority of these bacteria live in the intestines where they break down food into useful nutrients. The human mouth has its share of bacteria—more than 700 species. The bacteria live on gums, teeth, the lining of the mouth, and on the tongue.

The *Bacillus/Clostridium* group, the cyanobacteria group, and the spirochetes group offer a hint of the variety among the classic types of bacteria. From the human point of view, some of these microbes are crucial for life and some are deadly.

The *Bacillus/Clostridium* Group

This group includes the mycoplasmas, the clostridia, and the bacilli. Mycoplasmas are the smallest known bacteria. Since they lack a cell wall, mycoplasmas can take many shapes, including spheres and filaments. Mycoplasmas are widespread and live in soil, plants, and animals. Clostridia are anaerobic bacteria that form endospores. The tough endospores can contaminate food and germinate into active bacteria in food products. *Clostridium botulinum* produces one of the most potent biological toxins to affect humans and is one cause of food poisoning. Bacilli are rod-shaped bacteria that swim with twitching flagella. Many produce toxins that kill insects. Farmers spray the toxin on crops as a means of pest control. Certain bacilli are used in the food industry for producing fermented vegetables, beverages such as beer and wine, and products from milk including cheese and yogurt. Bacteria in the *Bacillus/Clostridium* group also inflict diseases in animals. Mycoplasmas cause pneumonia. *Bacillus* species produce anthrax disease and food poisoning. Clostridia cause tetanus, food poisoning, and gas gangrene.

The Cyanobacteria Group

Fossil evidence shows that oxygen-producing cyanobacteria have lived on Earth for at least 3.4 billion years. Scientists propose that cyanobacteria were probably the original source of oxygen in the atmosphere. The bacteria also convert atmospheric nitrogen into ammonia, nitrate, and other organic chemicals that plants need for growth. Today, cyanobacteria are one of the largest groups of bacteria and inhabit almost all waters and soils. Many cyanobacteria that live in surface layers of water have hollow protein structures filled with gas. They alter their depth by inflating or deflating the tiny gas bags. Most cyanobacteria have a pigmented coating.

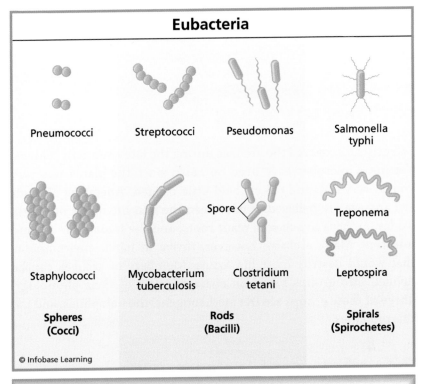

Eubacteria

Pneumococci

Streptococci

Pseudomonas

Salmonella typhi

Staphylococci

Mycobacterium tuberculosis

Spore

Clostridium tetani

Treponema

Leptospira

Spheres (Cocci)

Rods (Bacilli)

Spirals (Spirochetes)

© Infobase Learning

Figure 2.3   Eubacteria are unicellular microorganisms of various shapes. The shapes are called cocci (spherical), bacilli (rod-shaped), spirilla (spiral), and vibrios (broken spirals that look comma-shaped).

Depending upon the species, the coating appears blue, blue-black, green, gold, yellow, red, brown, or violet. Occasional overgrowth of reddish species of cyanobacteria inspired the naming of the Red Sea. Another reddish species is consumed by flamingos and colors the birds pink.

The Spirochetes Group

The spirochetes are slender, spiral-shaped bacteria, which have a unique feature: long flagella-like filaments embedded between the plasma membrane and a flexible external sheath. The filaments allow the bacteria to move through fluids, using a corkscrew motion. Spirochetes live in mud and sediment, as well as in the digestive tracts of insects, mollusks, and mammals. Some spirochetes cause Lyme disease, syphilis, and other disorders.

KINGDOM ARCHAEA: EXTREME MICROBES

Scientists discovered the archaea during the late twentieth century. Yet these microbes have lived on Earth since the planet was very young, very hot, and the air held little oxygen. Ancestors of modern archaea are believed to have been the first life forms on Earth. Today, archaea live in soil, plant roots, and the human mouth and intestine. Many archaea, however, thrive in harsh environments that would destroy most life forms. Members of archaea can be divided into groups based on characteristics of their physiology. Three of these groups are the methanogens, the halophiles, and the thermophiles.

The Methanogens ("Methane Makers")

Methanogens are anaerobes that consume carbon dioxide and hydrogen, and emit methane, the primary component of natural gas. These microbes live in oxygen-poor habitats, such as bogs, swamps, marshes, the ocean floor, animal intestines, and sewage treatment facilities. Methanogens produce most of the methane in the atmosphere. In wetlands, the methanogens are responsible for marsh gas. As they break down organic matter in flooded rice fields, methanogenic microbes emit tons of methane gas. Methanogens that live in animal intestines get the credit for the methane content of digestive gas. Thanks to methane-producing life forms that live in its stomach, a cow burps about 211 cups (50 liters) of methane every day.

The Halophiles ("Salt-loving")

These cells can thrive in liquid 10 times saltier than ocean water. Halophiles can be found in Utah's Great Salt Lake, the Dead Sea in the Middle East, and in artificial evaporation ponds. These archaea do not just tolerate high salt, they need the salt to survive.

The Thermophiles ("Heat-loving")

Thermophiles live at unusually high temperatures, such as the hot springs of Yellowstone National Park in Wyoming and thermal vents

Cavity-Fighting Gummy Bears?

During the seventeenth century, Antonie van Leeuwenhoek discovered that white, gooey matter scraped from his teeth teemed with bacteria. The sticky film that coated his teeth was plaque, which is formed by bacteria, acids, saliva, and food particles. As bacteria digest sugar in bits of food, they create acid that attacks minerals in enamel, the outer surface of the tooth. The small holes that form in enamel are cavities. After destroying enamel, acids continue to eat through the layers of the tooth until bacteria reach nerves and blood vessels. Then it is time for a trip to the dentist.

Proper care of teeth decreases the effects of acid-producing bacteria. Studies in the early 1990s revealed a further tactic in the fight against tooth decay: chewing gum that contains xylitol. Xylitol is a sweetener that looks and tastes like sugar. Bacteria that live in the mouth have a difficult time breaking down xylitol and produce only slight amounts of acid. In fact, bacteria expend so much energy trying to consume xylitol that they have little energy left over to reproduce themselves. So, the bacterial population decreases as old bacteria die. Chewing xylitol gum also stimulates saliva production. Saliva helps to flush bacteria from teeth.

In 2008, scientists reported that gummy bears containing xylitol may also fight tooth decay. Elementary school students volunteered to eat gummy bears during school hours. They chewed four gummy bears, three times a day. After six weeks, scientists examined plaque that coated the teeth of gummy bear–snacking students. They found that the bears had reduced the numbers of cavity-causing bacteria in these students' mouths.

Figure 2.4   An aerial view of the Great Salt Lake in Utah shows rich communities of salt-loving microbes called halophiles, which contain cell membranes colored by carotenoid compounds that appear as a reddish color.

in the ocean floor. The microbes grow in temperatures higher than 113° Fahrenheit (45° Centigrade). Some extreme forms, called hyperthermophiles, live in environments hotter than 212°F (100°C), the temperature at which water boils at sea level. One type of hyperthermophile, known as "strain 121," lives in water heated to 250°F (121°C). Scientists discovered the bacteria living in a volcanic sea vent in the northeast Pacific Ocean at a depth of 7,447 feet (2,270 meters). Most thermophiles require sulfur for their survival.

Some archaea combine physiological characteristics, such as the need for high salt and very hot temperatures. Certain archaea prefer

Energy from Microbes

Scientists have been searching for new sources of fuel to replace vanishing supplies of oil, coal, and other fossil fuels. In their quest for new sources of energy, scientists hunted for microbes that thrive in Iceland's geothermal hot springs. They found thermophiles that consumed glucose and other carbohydrates, and excreted hydrogen and ethanol, which may supplement common fossil fuels. One day, bacteria may produce these two fuels from wastewater of factories that process sugar beets, potatoes, and other plant materials.

Ethanol and hydrogen are not the only sources of energy produced by bacteria. *Shewanella* are a type of bacteria that live in water and soil. They devour simple organic compounds and produce electricity. Scientists have made tiny fuel cells powered by living *Shewanella*. However, a great deal of research will be required before a car or a house can be powered by microbes.

very low temperatures. Studies with cold-loving archaea microbes have shown that they can survive in temperatures below freezing, which are the types of temperatures found on Mars. Scientists suggest that an understanding of archaea can give clues about how life forms may survive on other planets or moons of the solar system.

3

Protists

The kingdoms of the eubacteria and the archaea contain single-cell life forms that are prokaryotes. The term *prokaryote* means "before nuts," which makes little sense by itself. The "nut" is not an actual nut, but instead refers to a nucleus, a structure that contains most of a cell's genetic material. A prokaryote is a simple cell that lacks a nucleus. A eukaryote ("true nuts") is a cell that contains a nucleus. Since prokaryotes appeared on Earth before eukaryotes with their nuclei, prokaryotes are "before nuts."

The life forms of the Kingdom Protista are eukaryotes. Some scientists say that Protista is a catchall group that includes any eukaryote that is not a fungus, plant, or animal. It is true that Protista encompasses a very diverse group of life forms. Certain protists survive by consuming simple chemicals, while others survive by eating living cells. Although many of the protists are microscopic in size, one type of protist, brown algae, can grow to about 98 to 262 feet (about 30 to 80 meters). Some protists resemble animal cells, others seem more like plant cells, and other protists resemble fungi.

MEET THE FAMILY OF PROTISTS
Family History: Development of Eukaryotes from Prokaryotes

A prokaryotic cell has three layers: an inner core of jelly-like cytoplasm, a plasma membrane, and an outer, rigid cell wall. The

Figure 3.1 Brown algae, shown in this micrograph, is primarily a large group of multicellular marine algae, including many types of seaweed.

cytoplasm contains deoxyribonucleic acid (DNA), ribonucleic acid (RNA), proteins, and other chemicals that the cell needs to survive and reproduce. Scientists propose that about 2 billion years ago, more complex cells evolved from prokaryotic cells. Over time, the plasma membrane extended into the cell to form compartments that divide tasks among small organ-like structures called organelles. One membrane compartment is the endoplasmic reticulum, a collection of folded membranes. It is here that the cell synthesizes many proteins.

Just as a cell has an outer plasma membrane, a membrane called the nuclear envelope surrounds the cell's nucleus. The nucleus stores genetic material that instructs the cell to make proteins. Pores in the nuclear envelope allow special RNA molecules to slip outside the nucleus and into the cytoplasm. These **messenger RNA** molecules carry instructions from the genetic material to the protein-making machinery. The instructions of the genetic material are stored in DNA. Typically, the DNA in a nucleus can be found in **chromatin**, a mixture of DNA and proteins. Under the microscope, chromatin has a wiry, fuzzy appearance. When a cell is getting ready to reproduce itself, the chromatin compacts into the form of **chromosomes**.

Mitochondria and **chloroplasts** are organelles that might have developed from a complex sequence of membrane folding. According to one popular theory, however, ancient eukaryotic cells obtained these organelles from small, invading prokaryotic cells. Prokaryotes called **endosymbionts** are key elements to this theory. A **symbiont** is an organism that forms a relationship with an organism of another species. Often, the relationship benefits both organisms. An endosymbiont is an organism that lives within the cell of another organism. The endosymbiont theory proposes that a large cell engulfed a smaller prokaryotic cell. Instead of eating the prokaryotic cell, the two cells formed a symbiotic relationship. The association benefitted both cells. The prokaryotic cell gained a stable environment inside the large cell. In return, the prokaryotic cell produced energy-rich chemicals for the large cell. The prokaryotic cell could provide this benefit because it was an aerobic and heterotrophic cell. That is, the prokaryotic cell needed oxygen to survive (aerobic), and the prokaryotic cell obtained nutrients from other living things (heterotrophic). The prokaryotic cell converted the nutrients into other useful chemicals. In time, the endosymbionts became jelly bean–shaped organelles that use oxygen to break down fats and sugars to synthesize high-energy chemicals that the eukaryotic cell uses to perform various functions. These organelles are mitochondria—they are the cell's powerhouses.

According to the endosymbiotic theory, a photosynthetic endosymbiont developed into another type of organelle: the chloroplast. Chloroplasts trap solar energy and use the energy to produce complex sugar molecules, high-energy chemicals, and oxygen from water and carbon dioxide. This chemical reaction is photosynthesis. While most eukaryotic cells contain many mitochondria, chloroplasts are found in eukaryotic cells capable of photosynthesis.

Various forms of evidence support the endosymbiont theory. For example, mitochondria and chloroplasts are about the right size for descendants of eubacteria. Also, both organelles have their own molecules of circular DNA that encode proteins required by the organelles to function.

Another important part of a eukaryotic cell is the cytoskeleton, which provides structure (like a skeleton) and movement (like

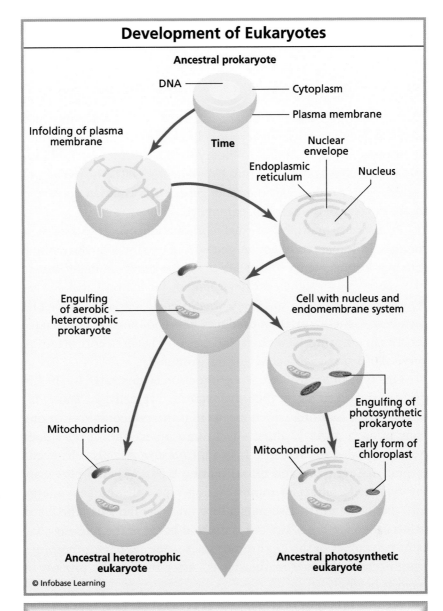

Development of Eukaryotes

Ancestral prokaryote

DNA

Cytoplasm

Plasma membrane

Time

Infolding of plasma membrane

Nuclear envelope

Endoplasmic reticulum

Nucleus

Engulfing of aerobic heterotrophic prokaryote

Cell with nucleus and endomembrane system

Engulfing of photosynthetic prokaryote

Mitochondrion

Mitochondrion

Early form of chloroplast

Ancestral heterotrophic eukaryote

Ancestral photosynthetic eukaryote

© Infobase Learning

Figure 3.2 According to one theory, the development of eukaryotes depended upon the infolding of the plasma membrane and the aquisition of useful prokaryotes.

muscles). The cytoskeleton is composed of long proteins. These protein cables create tracks that allow molecules and organelles to move within a cell. The proteins also help to form extensions of the cell membrane that enable certain cells to move and change into different shapes.

Reproduction Methods of the Protists

Prokaryotes reproduce by binary fission. A cell divides into two identical daughter cells. Eukaryotic cells, such as protists, reproduce by **mitosis**, which is similar to binary fission. In mitosis, a cell duplicates its DNA and divides into two daughter cells. The nucleus of each daughter cell carries the same genetic information contained by the nucleus of the original, parent cell.

Protists also multiply by sexual reproduction, using the process of **meiosis**. In sexual reproduction, genes from two individuals combine into new arrangements. The ability to shuffle genes among members of a species was a significant development for life on Earth. Sexual reproduction enables a species to create genetic variation among its members. Genetic variation produces new combinations of characteristics in offspring. New characteristics may become critical for the survival of a species in a changing environment.

One type of protist sexual reproduction is illustrated by the life cycle of the green algae, *Chlamydomonas*. Typically, a *Chlamydomonas* cell is **haploid**, which means that the cell contains just one copy of each of its 17 different chromosomes. This species does not have males and females. Instead, *Chlamydomonas* cells occur in plus mating types and minus mating types. When a plus mating type cell contacts a minus mating type cell, the cells merge into one cell and the two nuclei fuse into one nucleus. The fused cell is called a zygote. The cell is **diploid** because the nucleus contains two copies of the 17 chromosomes—one set of chromosomes from each of the two mating types. After fusion, the process of meiosis begins.

Meiosis proceeds in two stages to create four haploid daughter cells. In the first stage, DNA duplicates to produce twice the number of chromosomes. At this point, the nucleus contains one pair of 17 chromosomes from the plus mating type cell and one pair of 17 chromosomes from the minus mating type cell. After the nuclear membrane breaks down, web-like proteins attach to chromosomes,

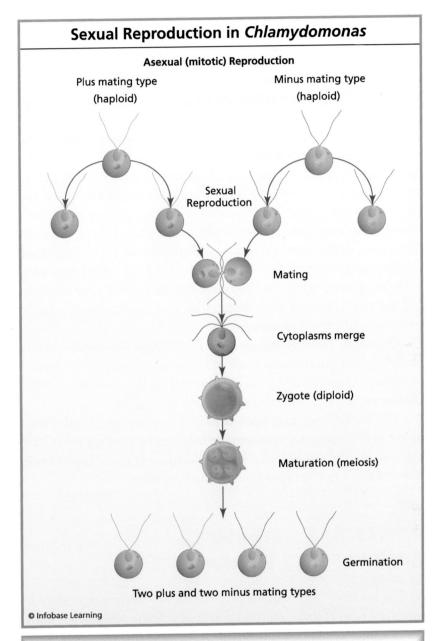

Sexual Reproduction in *Chlamydomonas*

Asexual (mitotic) Reproduction

Plus mating type
(haploid)

Minus mating type
(haploid)

Sexual
Reproduction

Mating

Cytoplasms merge

Zygote (diploid)

Maturation (meiosis)

Germination

Two plus and two minus mating types

© Infobase Learning

Figure 3.3 Unicellular flagellates called *Chlamydomonas* are often considered model organisms for molecular biology. This illustration shows how they can reproduce sexually.

and the proteins pull the chromosomes to two sides of the cell. Each side of the cell gets one pair of 17 chromosomes that are a mixture of chromosomes from the plus and minus mating type cells. The cell divides to produce two daughter cells.

Here is another way to think about the first stage of meiosis. Suppose that *Chlamydomonas* has only one type of chromosome called chromosome 1. A diploid zygote cell would have two copies of the chromosome—one from the plus mating type cell and one from the minus mating type cell. Call them chromosome 1p and chromosome 1m. The zygote gets ready to divide, and DNA duplicates. Now, the cell contains two copies of chromosome 1p and two copies of chromosome 1m. Each side of the cell gets two copies of chromosome 1. However, one side gets two copies of chromosome 1p, and the other side gets two copies of chromosome 1m. After the cell divides, each of the daughter cells has two copies of chromosome 1. One daughter cell has two copies of chromosome 1p, and one daughter cell has two copies of chromosome 1m.

Of course, *Chlamydomonas* has 17 different chromosomes and each daughter cell contains a pair of 17 chromosomes. Some of those chromosome pairs came from the plus mating type, and some of the chromosome pairs came from the minus mating type.

The second stage of meiosis is simple. Each daughter cell divides its set of chromosome pairs equally between two cells, so that each cell contains the same DNA. The four daughter cells are haploid cells that contain a new arrangement of chromosomes.

PROTISTS: A DIVERSE GROUP OF LIFE FORMS

Variety is a chief feature of the protists. All protists can reproduce by mitosis, but only some reproduce sexually. Some protists are **autotrophs,** capable of making nutrients from inorganic materials. Some protists are **heterotrophs,** deriving nutrition by degrading material of other cells. Some heterotrophs are scavengers. Other heterotrophs are hunters, engulfing their prey like the monster in *The Blob* movies, or shooting their victims with poison darts. These deadly hunters can be found in the Protozoa.

Animal-Like Protists

Protozoa live in the sea, freshwater, soil, decaying organic matter, and in plants and animals. Like animals, protozoa are heterotrophs, they can move, and they lack a cell wall. Bacteria are the favorite food of the protozoa. Bacteria alter the environment in ways that allow the survival of other life forms. For example, soil-dwelling bacteria remove atoms from inorganic sources and use them to produce organic materials that enrich the soil for plant growth. While bacteria play a vital role, an uncontrolled growth of bacteria would harm the environment. Protozoa consume bacteria and control their numbers.

Protozoa can be grouped according to the way that they travel through their microscopic worlds. These groups are the amoebas, the flagellates, the ciliates, and the sporozoans.

An amoeba moves by causing its cytoplasm to flow toward its objective. Flowing cytoplasm can extend from the main body in the form of pseudopods ("false feet"). Amoebas also use their pseudopods to engulf their prey. In a way, amoebas eat with their feet. The amoeba completely surrounds its food, enclosing the food in a membrane-bound vesicle, a food vacuole. Small vesicles called lysosomes fuse with the food vacuole and release enzymes that digest the food.

The flagellates use several long flagella to move in search of prey. The flagellum of protozoa is more complex than the flagellum of bacteria. In protozoa, the flagellum is part of the cytoskeleton system. Each flagellum has nine pairs of protein tubes called microtubules. The nine pairs of microtubules surround a central pair of microtubules. An extension of the plasma membrane covers the 9+2 set of microtubules, and a structure called a basal body anchors a flagellum to the cell. Not all flagellates are heterotrophs. Some are autotrophs that have chloroplasts and can obtain nutrients by photosynthesis.

The bodies of the ciliates are covered with rows of cilia, tiny threadlike structures similar to flagella. Cilia bend in the same direction, creating a wavelike motion that propels the cell through a watery environment. Certain ciliates are equipped with weapons. When threatened or hunting prey, the cells shoot threadlike darts that paralyze with a toxin. Another odd feature of ciliates is that they

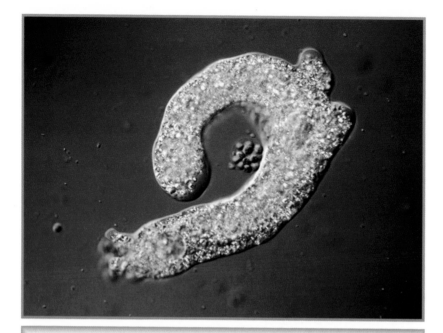

Figure 3.4 An amoeba surrounds green algae with its pseudopods.

maintain their genetic material in two types of nuclei: macronuclei and smaller micronuclei. The micronuclei appear to contain typical chromosomes, whereas the macronuclei contain a large number of clusters of DNA and protein. Macronuclei contain genes that control cell functions, whereas the genes of micronuclei are only needed for aspects of sexual reproduction unique to ciliates. A ciliate usually has more than one of each type of nucleus.

Lacking flagella or cilia, a sporozoan moves by bending its body and gliding. Most sporozoans are **parasites** that live in host cells. One type of sporozoan, *Plasmodium*, causes malaria in humans. Mosquitoes carry *Plasmodium* parasites, which are injected into the human body with the mosquito's saliva when the insect bites. One type of *Plasmodium* enters a human body, invades liver cells, reproduces, and then invades red blood cells. Here, they feed on hemoglobin—the protein that carries oxygen from the lungs—and they reproduce again. The new parasites destroy red blood cells when they burst from the cells.

Plant-Like Protists

Algae are a group of diverse life forms that vary from single-celled organisms to huge colonies of cells. Most algae have cell walls and use chloroplasts to obtain energy from photosynthesis. In this way, algae are like plants. The algae can be grouped by the color of pigment in their chloroplasts: yellow-brown (gold), red, brown, and green.

The golden algae, which live in fresh water, can switch between autotrophic and heterotrophic lifestyles. If light levels become too low to sustain photosynthesis, the algae become heterotrophs, feeding on bacteria and other algae. The golden algae typically move using two flagella attached near one end of the cell.

Red algae mainly live in the seas, and they vary from single-celled to multicellular forms. The larger types of red algae grow

Tracking a Giant Deep-Sea Protist

Mikhail Matz discovered an amazing life form roaming through the silt about 2,526 ft. (770 m) below the ocean surface. The University of Texas biologist had been diving with colleagues near the Bahamas when they saw small life forms in front of groove-like tracks on the seafloor. The creatures looked like dark-green grapes up to 1.18 inches (30 millimeters) in diameter. Close examination revealed that the creatures were single-celled protists covered with thin, clear walls. Matz suggested that the protists move by forming pseudopods that grab onto mud in one direction. The creature then rolls in that direction and leaves a track in the sediment. This is the first time that a single-celled life form has been found to create animal-like tracks.

Fossils that date as early as 1.8 billion years ago contain similar grooves. Scientists have interpreted the grooves as tracks made by ancient multicellular animals. The discovery of the giant protist suggests that a large, single-celled life form might have laid those tracks.

as branched filaments. Humans use the cell walls of red algae to fabricate a variety of products, including additives for baked goods, cosmetics, and drug capsules. Coralline red algae secrete a hard covering of carbonate and have contributed to the formation of tropical reefs for millions of years.

Brown algae, which are commonly known as seaweeds, are almost all marine-dwelling, multicellular organisms. Giant kelp belong to this group. Marine life forms eat brown algae and humans use the algae to produce animal feed, fertilizer, and many foods, such as candy and ice cream.

Green algae live as single-celled organisms, colonies of cells, and as multicellular life forms. *Chlamydomonas* is an example of a single-celled green alga. When the environment becomes unfavorable for the survival of *Chlamydomonas*, two haploid cells fuse to form a diploid zygote. The zygote forms a thick wall that protects the cell against hostile conditions. Sea lettuce is an example of a multicellular green alga. The ruffle-edged leaves, which can grow to about to 2 ft. (about 0.6 m), can be seen in coastal tidal pools.

The aquatic diatoms are another type of plant-like protist. They live as single cells, filaments, or colonies of cells. A diatom has a shell composed of two halves, called valves. The valves contain silica and have elaborate patterns of holes and slits. The numerous openings allow the passage of water and other molecules between the environment and the inner cell.

Fungus-Like Protists

Certain protists have features shared with fungi. The chytrids, for example, strengthen their cell walls with chitin, a complex sugar molecule. True fungi also produce chitin. Chytrids live in water and soil. They feed by extending threadlike tubes into organic debris, recently dead organisms, or living organisms. Then, they secrete digestive enzymes through the tubes to degrade organic matter and absorb the nutrients. Some chytrids live within the cells of a living organism.

The water molds have cell walls composed mainly of cellulose. Shaped like filaments, they absorb nutrients from the soil or water. Water molds also obtain food by invading plants, insects, fish, and other organisms. One water mold, *Phytophthora infestans*, kills

Figure 3.5   This arrangement of centric and pinnate diatoms is magnified. Each diatom has an intricately patterned cell wall, or frustule, made of silica and pectin.

potatoes by invading the stem and leaf tissues. During one week in 1846, the mold destroyed most of Ireland's potato crop. The mold caused the Great Famine, which led to the deaths of almost one million Irish by 1860.

Slime molds play an important role in the **ecosystem**—they decompose dead organisms and return chemical nutrients to the environment. Slime molds occur in a plasmodial form and in a cellular form. In the plasmodial stage of its life cycle, a plasmodial slime mold has the form of a very large single cell with thousands of diploid nuclei. Some of these plasmodia slither under the bark of rotting trees or under leaves, engulfing food like amoeba. If the environment becomes unfavorable to the plasmodia, the organism produces haploid spores that are dispersed. The spores develop into amoeba-like cells and cells with flagella. These single cells can fuse to create a diploid zygote that develops into a plasmodium. Cellular slime molds have the form of amoebas until food becomes scarce. Then, they aggregate to create an organism that looks like a plasmodium. Unlike a

Diatoms and the Icehouse Effect

A typical greenhouse is a small, glass building used to grow plants. Greenhouses keep plants warm because the glass panels allow light to enter, but prevent heat from leaving. The "greenhouse effect" refers to the rise in world temperature by gases, such as carbon dioxide. These greenhouse gases trap energy from the Sun like the glass panels in a greenhouse. If the air lacked greenhouse gases, Earth would be about 60°F (about 15.6°C) cooler. Today, scientists warn about global warming. A warming trend might be caused in part by the burning of fossil fuels that has increased the amounts of carbon dioxide in the air. In the past, Earth has experienced severe global cooling due to an "icehouse effect"—that is, a large drop of atmospheric carbon dioxide levels allowed the Sun's heat to escape from the planet.

A recent study suggests that, millions of years ago, the humble diatom might have caused an icehouse effect. During photosynthesis, diatoms convert carbon dioxide into organic carbon. The ocean's diatoms remove billions of tons of carbon dioxide from the air every year. An analysis of the fossil record indicates that the number of diatom species rapidly increased and then abruptly declined about 33 million years ago. In the ancient seas, the explosion of diatom populations could have resulted in a depletion of atmospheric carbon dioxide that triggered an icehouse effect and severe global cooling.

true plasmodium, the colony is composed of cells that retain their plasma membranes.

PARTING WITH THE PROTISTS

Compared with the prokaryotes, the eukaryotic protists are a very complex form of life. Protist cells have membrane compartments to separate vital functions, such as protein synthesis, degradation of nutrients, and storage of the **genome**. A genome is the complete set of an organism's genes. Protists also have mitochondria and chloroplasts to power cellular functions. Kingdom Protista includes cells with organelles and other features found in the cells of animals, plants, and fungi. Protist lifestyles vary from autotrophs to heterotrophs, from single cells to colonies, and from free living cells to intracellular parasites. Yet the protists seem simple compared with multicellular eukaryotes.

Fungi

L ike the Kingdom Protista, the Kingdom Fungi includes a diverse group of eukaryotic life forms. Mushrooms, mildews, rusts, and yeasts reside in the fungi kingdom. So far, scientists have found about 100,000 species of fungi, but at least 10 times that number may exist. Some fungi are microscopic in size, while others are huge. Scientists discovered a honey mushroom living three feet (0.9 meter) underground in the Malheur National Forest in eastern Oregon. The fungus weighs hundreds of tons and covers 2,200 acres (890 hectares). The mushroom has been growing for at least 2,400 years and is the largest living life form ever found.

INTRODUCTION TO FUNGI

With several exceptions, fungi are almost entirely multicellular. The fossil record shows that fungi have lived on Earth for about 900 million years. Although fungi first evolved in water, they developed the ability to live on land, where they have thrived. Today, fungi rank as one of most widely distributed life forms on the planet. Fungi vary greatly in appearance. Yet they share two common characteristics. One characteristic is that they grow through a structure called mycelium.

The structure of a fungus can be examined at four levels, from the microscopic to the macroscopic:

Figure 4.1 A honey mushroom in eastern Oregon's Malheur National Forest has been spreading its black shoestring filaments, called rhizomorphs, through the forest for about 2,400 years. The only above-ground evidence of the giant fungus are clusters of golden mushrooms that pop up each fall.

Cells

↓

Tubular filaments (hypha or hyphae)

↓

Mass of hyphae (mycelium or mycelia)

↓

Fungus body (thallus)

A typical fungus consists of a collection of tubular filaments. Each filament—called a hypha (plural: hyphae)—is enclosed by a cell wall strengthened with chitin. The cell wall surrounds the plasma membrane and cytoplasm. The tube of a hypha may be divided by septa. Septa are like walls that divide a hypha into compartments. Septa usually have pores that allow passage of molecules and even organelles. Some fungi lack septa and have hyphae filled with cytoplasm containing hundreds or thousands of nuclei. A fungus produces proteins and other chemicals that stream through the cytoplasm toward the tips of their hyphae. By extending their bodies from hyphae tips, fungi move into new areas, searching for food. A mass of hyphae branch into a network called the mycelium (plural: mycelia). The mycelium composes the body of a fungus, which is called the thallus.

The second common characteristic of fungi concerns their method of obtaining nutrition. Fungi absorb organic matter from other organisms, both alive and dead. This method of feeding differs from that found in the animal and plant kingdoms. Fungi break down their food by secreting digestive enzymes onto organic material. Then they absorb nutrient molecules through the hyphae. As they decompose organic matter, fungi return nitrogen-rich compounds to the soil, where they are used by plants. Like heterotrophic bacteria, fungi play an important role in the environment as organisms that decompose and recycle nutrients. Sometimes, hungry fungi create trouble for humans. Fungi readily break down leather, fuel, cloth, paint, and electrical insulation, as well as meats, breads, fruits, and vegetables.

Some fungi secrete enzymes that break down the walls of plant cells. This allows the fungus to absorb nutrients from plant cells through a type of special hypha called a haustorium. Not all of the plant-invading fungi are parasitic. Some exchange nutrients with plant cells in a mutually beneficial relationship.

Members of the Kingdom Fungi multiply by asexual reproduction and sexual reproduction. Most fungi reproduce asexually by forming spores that enable a fungus to spread throughout its environment. As a mycelium matures, it may form a fruiting body, which is also called a sporophore. Usually, the fruiting body is the part of a fungus that is visible above ground. The fruiting body produces spores that are released into the environment, where they are carried by wind and water. Sometimes, fungi give their spores a boost. Certain fungi have fruiting bodies that launch trillions of spores in a burst. Spores germinate after landing on a moist surface that

Fungi Structures

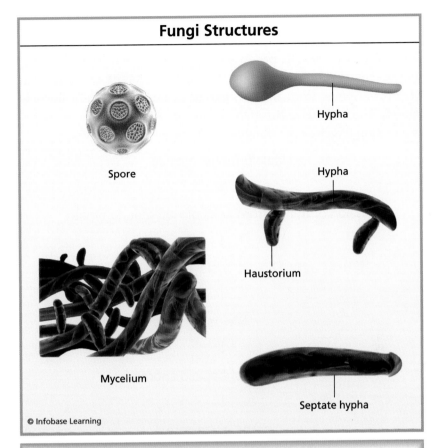

Spore

Hypha

Hypha

Haustorium

Mycelium

Septate hypha

© Infobase Learning

Figure 4.2 There is a great deal of variety in the size, structure, and complexity of various fungi.

has nutrients. Then, hyphae develop from the germinating spores, branch, and become the mycelium of a new fungus.

Three stages of sexual reproduction begin when mycelia of different mating types meet and fuse. In a stage called plasmogamy, two mycelia with haploid nuclei fuse to combine cytoplasm. The two nuclei fuse during karyogamy, resulting in the formation of a diploid nucleus. The nucleus contains one set of chromosomes from each of the original two cells. The diploid cell is a zygote. Meiosis proceeds in a way unique to fungi. In other eukaryotes, the membrane of the nucleus breaks down to allow separation of chromosomes. In fungi, the nuclear membrane remains intact. Web-like proteins separate chromosomes within the nucleus, which then pinches to form two haploid nuclei. Meiosis produces haploid cells that have the same number of chromosomes, but they have different combinations of chromosomes from the two parent cells. Haploid cells become spores, which disperse throughout the environment. The sexual reproduction life cycle of a fungus can be outlined as follows:

Haploid fungal hyphae

↓

Fusion of nuclei from cells of two mating types

↓

Diploid nuclei form

↓

Meiosis

↓

Formation of haploid spores

↓

Spores germinate

↓

Haploid fungal hyphae

Fungi alternate between haploid and diploid phases. In most fungi, only the zygote is diploid and the other cells are haploid.

A TOUR OF FUNGUS TYPES

Fungi can be grouped by differences in their methods of reproduction. The four key groups are the ascomycetes, the basidiomycetes, the zygomycetes, and the glomeromycetes.

The Ascomycetes

With at least 65,000 species, the ascomycetes group may include about 75% of fungal types. Members vary from cup fungi, truffles, morels, and other multicellular fungi to single-celled yeasts. The ascomycetes, or sac fungi, play an important role in recycling organic matter. The group also includes fungi that inflict infections and diseases in plants, animals, and humans. Humans have found uses for many of the sac fungi. For example, the yeast *Saccharomyces cerevisiae* is used to prepare bread and in the brewing of alcoholic beverages. Some sac fungi synthesize life-saving antibiotics.

Most sac fungi reproduce asexually by forming spores from structures at the tips of modified hyphae called conidiophores. The

Fungi Clean the Environment

A network of fungal mycelia quietly labors within topsoil, recycling nutrients from plant and animal debris. Fungi are natural decomposers. Can fungi help humans to tidy up their messes?

Scientists are seeking ways to use fungi to clean man-made pollutants. Fungi may be able to degrade toxic chemicals in fertilizers, pesticides, explosives, oil, and industrial wastes. This method of removing toxins would be safe and would require little human effort. Dirt chock-full of toxic chemicals would be purified to produce compost or clean soil.

Researchers at the Pacific Northwest National Laboratory tested more than 50 types of fungi to identify organisms with the ability to break down certain toxins. To test the pollution-degrading fungi, scientists collected soil from the earthen floor of a building used to store vehicles, soil contaminated with diesel oil, and soil tainted with gasoline. They added mushrooms to four-foot (1.2-m) mounds of polluted soil samples. Then they waited. About five weeks later, mushroom fruiting bodies appeared above ground. Some of the mushrooms reached 12 inches (about 30 centimeters) in diameter. Below the surface, mycelia networks had penetrated throughout the soil. The scientists realized that the soil no longer reeked of oil. After four months, the mushrooms had so thoroughly cleaned the soil that it could be used for landscaping.

spores are known as conidia. Sexual reproduction starts with the fusion of hyphae from two different mating types of sac fungi. A structure forms that gives this group of fungi their name: the sac-like ascus in a fruiting body. In the ascus, plasmogamy, karyogamy, and meiosis produce ascospores, which are haploid spores. Most of the sac fungi can blast their ascospores into the air to be carried by the wind.

The yeast members of the sac fungi live as single cells. To reproduce sexually, yeast cells form an ascus, which is why yeasts are grouped with the multicellular sac fungi. Yeasts reproduce asexually using mitosis to divide into two cells. A simple version of the process is fission, which is similar to the binary fission used by bacteria. Mitosis can also lead to reproduction by budding. This process begins with the weakening of an area of the cell wall. Tension within the cell causes cytoplasm to push against the weak cell wall and form a bud. As the bud expands, mitosis produces a second nucleus, which moves into the new cell. When the budding cell reaches a certain size, cell wall material is produced to seal the connection between the two cells. The process leaves a scar on the surface of the parent cell. Scientists can determine the age of a yeast cell by counting the number of bud scars on the cell surface.

Many species of sac fungi live with green algae or cyanobacteria in a symbiotic relationship that benefits both types of life forms. The combination of a photosynthetic microbe and a fungus is a lichen. Most of the mass of a lichen is formed by the fungus, which provides the lichen with its general shape. The fungus offers its photosynthetic partner a stable, safe environment and secretes acids that help the microbes to obtain minerals. The green algae or cyanobacteria usually dwell in a layer below the lichen's surface where they produce organic nutrients for the fungus.

Lichens live on roofs, rotting logs, rocks, and tree bark. They thrive in the frigid Antarctic and Arctic, the scorching tropics, and in the thin air of mountains. Lichens are hardy life forms, but air pollution is deadly for them because they absorb toxins from the air. The death of lichens in an area signals declining air quality.

The Basidiomycetes

The basidiomycetes group includes about 30,000 species. Known as the club fungi, they have fruiting bodies familiar as mushrooms, puffballs,

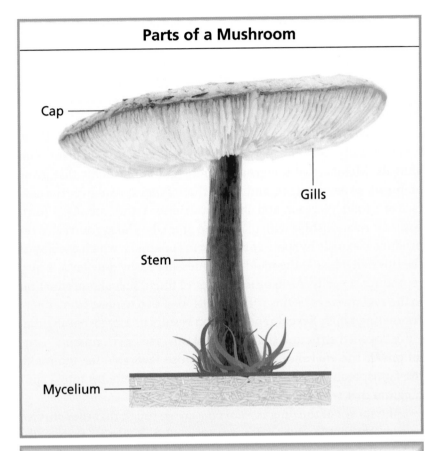

Parts of a Mushroom

Cap

Gills

Stem

Mycelium

Figure 4.3 A mushroom has an underground part, called the mycelium, and an above ground part, which is the reproductive organ and may be edible.

stinkhorns, and toadstools. The club fungi are efficient decomposers of wood. All club fungi are heterotrophs, and some form symbiotic relationships with shrubs and forest trees. These symbiotic fungi produce a sheath of hyphae around the root and secrete hormones that stimulate the root to branch. Fungi transfer nitrogen and other basic nutrients to the plant and take complex sugars from the plant. Other club fungi—the smuts and rusts—form parasitic relationships with plants and destroy food crops, such as corn and wheat.

During sexual reproduction, club fungi produce haploid basidiospores in a basidium, a club-shaped cell. The fruiting body of a mushroom can release a billion basidiospores. The spores drop through slits (called gills) in the fruiting body's cap, and winds carry the spores to new land.

The Zygomycetes

Scientists have found about 1,000 species of the zygomycetes. These fungi typically consume materials from dead or decaying plants and animals. Members of the group include common molds that grow on bread, sweet potatoes, and fruit. These fungi spread over the surface of a food, pierce it, and absorb nutrients. Other members form parasitic relationships with plants and animals. The zygomycetes reproduce asexually by spores produced in sporangia, which develop at the tips of hyphae. If the mold consumes all nearby nutrients, it may reproduce sexually. As in other groups of fungi, sexual reproduction in the zygomycetes begins with the fusion of two hyphae from different mating types. Sexual reproduction results in a zygosporangium, a thick-walled structure that can resist adverse environmental conditions. If the environment becomes more favorable for the mold, the zygosporangium undergoes meiosis and germinates into a sporangium that releases spores.

The spores of the fungus *Pilobolus* are so tough that they survive passage through a cow. After exiting a cow, *Pilobolus* germinates and breaks down materials in the dung. The fungus faces a problem when it is time to disperse its spores. *Pilobolus* must place its spores in grass, so that a cow will eat them while grazing. To give the spores a chance at a new life in fresh cow dung, *Pilobolus* grows a stalk that has spores on the top. The stalk has a light-sensitive area that causes *Pilobolus* to grow facing the sun. Water pressure builds in the stalk until the tip explodes, propelling spores toward the light, where plants are probably growing. The explosion is sufficient to blast spores eight feet (2.4 meters) away.

The Glomeromycetes

The glomeromycetes group is very old. Fossil evidence indicates that glomeromycetes have lived on Earth for more than 450 million years. Today, the group is a small one—scientists have found fewer than 200 species. Glomeromycetes fungi may only reproduce

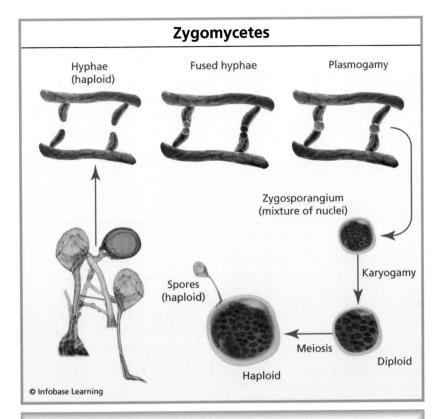

Zygomycetes

Hyphae (haploid)

Fused hyphae

Plasmogamy

Zygosporangium (mixture of nuclei)

Karyogamy

Spores (haploid)

Meiosis

Diploid

Haploid

© Infobase Learning

Figure 4.4 Zygomycetes fungi can reproduce asexually by spores or sexually by fusing two hyphae of different mating typse.

asexually. Asexual reproduction is achieved by spores or with fragments of hyphae that develop into new fungi.

Almost all members of this group are symbionts that form mutually beneficial relationships with plants. Hyphae enter plant root cells and form tree-shaped structures inside the cells. On the outside of the plant, the fungi serve as an additional root system. The fungus increases the supply of water and nutrients for the plant. In exchange, the fungus takes sugars produced by plant cells. About 70% to 90% of land plant species benefit from such a symbiotic relationship. Many members of the group are not only symbionts, they are obligate symbionts. This means that the fungi can only survive with a plant partner. Spores from an obligate symbiont must find a plant root to grow into a fungus.

Ants Farm Fungus

About 50 to 60 million years ago, ants became farmers in South America. They began to grow fungi. Today, more than 200 species of attine ants raise crops of fungi. The ants supply the fungi with nutrients and protect the fungi against disease-causing microbes. Usually, they grow a type of basidiomycetes fungus. Farming fungi is not a matter of choice for the ants. They depend upon the cultivation of fungus gardens for their food. When young ant queens leave their nest to begin new colonies, they carry a sample of fungus in their mouths and then use the bit of fungus to start their own food crop.

Attine ants grow their fungus gardens on organic debris. Leaf-cutting ants have developed a more-advanced approach to agriculture. They gather and process fresh leaves, flowers, and grasses. The harvest is not for the ants; leaf cutter ants cannot digest the plant matter. However, the ants grow fungi that degrade plant material into nutrients that the ants can digest.

FAREWELL TO FUNGI

At one time, scientists had classified fungi with plants. Yet fungi have characteristics distinct from traits found in plants. For example, the main component of fungal cell walls is chitin, a material found in insects and other animals. Plant cell walls contain cellulose, rather than chitin. Unlike plants, fungi eat by absorbing nutrients, and they grow by forming networks of hyphae. As scientists learned more about fungi, they decided that fungi deserve their own kingdom in the classification of life forms.

5

Plants

In a multicellular organism, functions required to survive and reproduce are divided among special groups of cells. Through a division of labor, specialized cells work together to ensure the life and continuity of the multicellular life form. Plants are multicellular organisms that use light as a source of energy. Scientists have identified more than 300,000 species of living plants. Another half million plant species may yet be discovered.

Scientists propose that plants evolved from ancestors of aquatic green algae. Modern green algae and plants still share many features. For example, both types of organisms have cell walls that contain the complex sugar cellulose. The cells of plants and green algae also use the same types of chlorophyll pigments to perform photosynthesis in chloroplasts. About 500 million years ago, plants moved from the aquatic lifestyle of green algae to life on land. The change offered more light and carbon dioxide to perform photosynthesis. As plants adapted to life on land, they acquired several new traits:

- Plant spores are covered with a complex chemical that protects the spore from dry air. Until they are released into the environment, spores are sheltered within a multicellular structure called the sporangium.
- The division of labor in multicellular plants led to the development of two types of cells: **gametes** and **somatic cells**. A gamete is an egg cell or a sperm cell. Both types

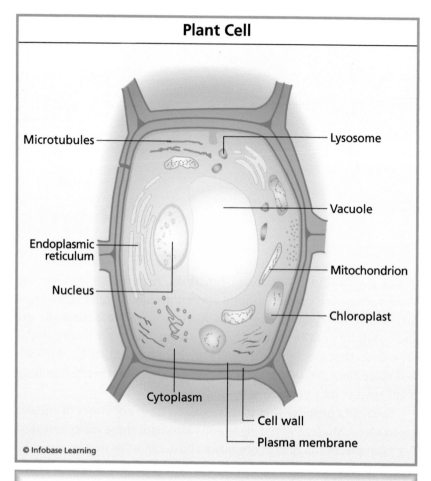

Plant Cell

Microtubules — Lysosome

Endoplasmic reticulum

Nucleus —

Vacuole

Mitochondrion

Chloroplast

Cytoplasm

Cell wall

Plasma membrane

© Infobase Learning

Figure 5.1 A plant cell includes a nucleus, cell wall, and chloroplasts.

of gametes are haploid cells. A somatic cell is a type of cell that makes up the body of an organism. In other words, a somatic cell is a cell other than an egg cell or a sperm cell. Plants produce gametes within the protected environment of an organ called the gametangia.

• In the process of fertilization, a sperm's nuclear DNA enters an egg cell and combines with the egg's nuclear DNA. The result is a zygote. In land plants, a zygote develops into an embryo within tissues of the female parent. Maternal tissues not only protect the embryo, but also supply nutrients. The dependency of a plant embryo on a parent is a significant change from the life of ancestral green algae. The evolution of the nurtured embryo enabled plants to thrive on dry land.

Aquatic organisms are surrounded by nutrients. Plants that live on land must obtain nutrients from the air and from the ground. Above the ground, plants obtain light energy and carbon dioxide, while soil provides minerals and water. In a search for nutrition, plants expand above and below the ground by growing from their apical meristems. Apical meristems are areas of active cell division found in roots and shoots. In most plants, shoot meristems produce leaves.

Most plants have a life cycle that varies between a generation of a plant with haploid cells and a plant generation with diploid cells. A haploid plant is called a gametophyte, whereas a diploid plant is termed a sporophyte. As the names suggest, a gametophyte plant produces gametes, and a sporophyte plant produces spores. A shift between haploid and diploid phases may seem familiar. Fungi alternate between haploid and diploid states. However, in most fungi, only a zygote cell is diploid; the other cells are haploid. Plants have a multicellular haploid form and a multicellular diploid form. A plant alternates between the two forms, as shown in the following generalized plant life cycle:

Multicellular sporophyte (diploid)

↓

Sporophyte produces haploid spores
by meiosis within a sporangium

↓

Spores germinate and develop into
multicellular haploid gametophytes

↓

Gametophytes use mitosis to produce
haploid gametes within gametangia

↓

Gametes fuse to form a diploid zygote

↓

Zygote develops into multicellular diploid sporophyte

Note several aspects of this process. A diploid sporophyte uses meiosis so that spore nuclei contain one copy of each chromosome (haploid), rather than two copies of each chromosome (diploid). Haploid spores develop into a haploid gametophyte. Since a gametophyte is haploid, it can produce haploid gametes by simple cell division, mitosis. Two haploid gametes fuse to form a diploid zygote. By the way, animals use meiosis to produce haploid gametes from diploid cells. Why are gametes haploid? If gametes were not haploid, then fusion of two gametes would produce a fused cell with twice the number of chromosomes found in a diploid cell. Chromosome numbers would continue to double with each animal generation or each round of sexual reproduction in plants.

The plant kingdom encompasses a diverse group of life forms. Some plants have sporophyte and gametophyte phases that look so different that they appear to belong to different species. The dominance of the plant life cycle phase varies as well. A dominant phase is one that lives longer and may be larger than the non-dominant phase. In some plants, the gametophyte phase is dominant, while other plants have a dominant sporophyte phase. Some plants have a gametophyte phase that is microscopic. All living plants probably evolved from ancestors that reproduced by the fusion of gametes to produce embryos. Yet many plants reproduce in other ways. For instance, strawberry plants reproduce asexually by growing horizontal stems that produce new plants.

Scientists have classified plants according to another variation: the presence or absence of a vascular system. Vascular plants have a system of tubes that transport nutrients and water throughout the plant. The main parts of the vascular system are the xylem and phloem. In the xylem, narrow, hollow cells convey water and minerals from the roots to the plant body. The xylem can also help to support the plant body as it grows above ground. A tree's wood is composed of xylem. Phloem cells transport nutrients in the opposite direction. Most plants have leaves with cells that produce sugars by photosynthesis. The phloem carries sugars and other nutrients from the leaves to the rest of the plant body. In brief, vascular plants have a transport system that functions in two directions:

Water and minerals (roots) → plant body ← sugars and other nutrients (leaves)

Figure 5.2 Strawberry plants grow runners, or stems, horizontally, which helps them reproduce asexually.

The evolution of a vascular system allowed plants to grow taller, expanding above the surface where they could gather more energy from sunlight. Plants that lack a vascular system—the nonvascular plants—grow close to the ground.

NONVASCULAR PLANTS

The first plants to live on land were probably nonvascular plants called bryophytes. These are simple plants, and scientists consider them primitive, compared with vascular plants. Since they lack a vascular system, bryophytes are small, usually reaching less than 5 inches (about 13 centimeters) in height. The plants can be found growing closely together in mats on the ground, logs, rocks, or trees. Bryophytes lack roots. Instead, delicate structures called rhizoids anchor the plants to a surface. Rhizoids are slender strands of cells or tubular single cells. Lacking the vascular tissue of roots, rhizoids do not play a major role in the absorption of minerals and water from the soil.

The gametophyte phase dominates the life cycle of nonvascular plants. Compared with sporophytes, gametophytes live longer and are larger. Sporophytes may be invisible to the naked eye, attached to parent gametophytes to absorb water and nutrients from them. Some bryophytes appear to lack a sporophyte phase. This type of bryophyte has gametophytes that can reproduce asexually—plant fragments grow into new gametophytes.

Many bryophytes are the first to colonize bare rock and contribute to soil development. They thrive in humid forests. In forests and bogs, bryophytes bind the soil and reduce erosion. Today, the bryophyte group includes about 16,000 species classified as mosses, hornworts, and liverworts. With its 10,000 species, the group of mosses has the greatest diversity among the bryophytes. These simple plants grow red-brown rhizoids, which anchor the moss, and the plant absorbs water and minerals with thin leaves. Hornworts have a sporophyte with a long, tapered shape, resembling a horn. These are often the first plant species to grow in an open area that has moist ground. Liverworts are named after their liver-shaped gametophytes.

VASCULAR PLANTS

Today, most land plants are vascular plants, which are usually larger and more complex than nonvascular plants. As previously discussed, the key trait of the vascular plants is a vascular system composed of xylem and phloem. Xylem cells have walls strengthened with lignin compounds, which are large chemicals that can also be found between cells and within cells. The compounds support the growth of plant stems above ground and fortify roots below the ground. Lignin enables trees to grow tall, and it also gives vegetables their crunch. Lignin is the second most abundant organic material on Earth; the most abundant material is also synthesized by plants: cellulose. The roots of vascular plants not only anchor a plant, but also play a vital role in transporting water and nutrients from the soil to the body of the plant. In addition to a vascular system and roots, most vascular plants have leaves that function as the main photosynthetic apparatus. Vascular plants also differ from nonvascular plants in their life cycles: They have a dominant sporophyte phase.

The huge group of vascular plants can be divided into those that produce seeds and those that do not. The oldest type of vascular plant is the seedless plant.

Nonseed Plants

About 350 million years ago, seedless vascular plants formed the first forests. Since they had vascular tissue, leaves, and roots, the plants also performed photosynthesis at an increased rate, removing more

Farmers Receive Text Message from Crops: Water Us!

Members of the plant kingdom can achieve many amazing things. Now, technology enables crops to send a request for water to farmers' cell phones.

A company called Accent Engineering, Inc. of Lubbock, Texas developed a drought monitoring system called SmartCrop. The system uses infrared thermometers to check the temperature of the surface of leaves in a field. A crop will suffer from drought if it is exposed to a certain temperature for a prolonged length of time. Consider cotton crops, for example. In northern Texas, cotton experiences effects of drought if the plants are exposed for over six and one-half hours to temperatures above 82° Fahrenheit (27.8° Celsius). With the SmartCrop system, each heat sensor collects information on leaf temperatures and data on the environment. Over 200 sensors broadcast their data to a computerized base station, located in the field. The base station computer analyzes the data and calculates whether heat stress threatens the crop. If so, the base station can send a signal to irrigate the crop. Alternatively, the base station can forward a text message to the farmer's cell phone. The farmer receives a "heat stress alert" with details about the threat that allows the farmer to decide about irrigation.

and more carbon dioxide from the air. As atmospheric carbon dioxide levels dropped, more sunlight escaped into space. Earth cooled and glaciers spread, marking a new ice age.

In ancient forests, ferns dominated plant life. They remain the most common seedless vascular plant. Most of a fern grows as an underground stem. Only divided leaves called fronds appear above the surface. A frond is also called a megaphyll, which means "large leaf," and this is one feature that distinguishes ferns from other seedless vascular plants. A frond consists of a leaf blade and a leaf stalk attached to an underground stem.

Ferns reproduce sexually and asexually. During the life cycle of a fern, diploid sporophyte plants produce haploid spores, usually on the underside of fronds. The spores are ejected from the fronds and carried by the wind. Spores germinate and produce a small, heart-shaped gametophyte plant that is haploid and varies in thickness from one to several cells. The gametophyte produces egg cells and sperm cells. Sperm fertilize an egg cell and produce a diploid zygote, which then develops into an embryo that absorbs nutrients from the gametophyte. The gametophyte dies soon after the embryo has matured into a sporophyte. In asexual reproduction, underground stems branch and grow a cluster of fronds above the surface. If the underground stem breaks, severing the connection between the frond cluster and the parent plant, then the frond cluster continues to grow as a separate plant.

Seed Vascular Plants

The hallmark trait of seed plants is the seed, which consists of a plant embryo with a supply of food. Seeds are covered with a protective coat that shelters the embryo from environmental hazards. In contrast to spores of nonseed plants, seeds can remain inactive for years until conditions are favorable for germination. Seed plants also have the following traits:

- **Reduced gametophyte phase in the life cycle**: Unlike seedless plants, seed plants typically have microscopic gametophytes. The gametophytes are so small that they can be protected within the tissues of the sporophyte.

- **Heterospory**: Seed plants produce two types of spores: megaspores and microspores. Megaspores mature into female gametophytes, whereas microspores mature into male gametophytes. Female gametophytes produce eggs, and male gametophytes produce sperm. In contrast, most nonseed plants produce one type of spore that develops into a gametophyte, which produces both egg cells and sperm cells.
- **Pollen**: A grain of pollen contains a male gametophyte. Pollen grains are coated with a durable wall that protects the gametophyte. Seedless vascular plants and nonvascular plants produce sperm cells that must use flagella to swim in a layer of water to fertilize egg cells. This reflects methods used by ancient marine ancestors of plants. Pollen does not require water and can safely travel great distances.
- **Ovules**: An ovule is a structure that protects a megaspore, which matures into a female gametophyte that produces an egg. An opening in the protective coating of the ovule allows a pollen grain to enter. The pollen contains a male gametophyte that ejects sperm, which fertilize the egg. After fertilization, the ovule develops into a seed to protect the embryo.

Scientists divide the many seed plants into two groups: gymnosperms and angiosperms. Gymnosperms are vascular seed plants that do not make flowers, and angiosperms are flowering plants.

Gymnosperms produce seed on modified leaves. Typically, the leaves are arranged as cones. The gymnosperm group contains the longest-living forms of life on the planet. It also includes some of the largest life forms. Redwoods, pines, spruce, and ginkgos are gymnosperms, as are many vines and shrubs. The group includes about 700 living species.

Angiosperms produce seeds in an ovary, a structure that develops into a fruit. With more than 300,000 known living species, flowering plants are the largest and most diverse group of plants. The angiosperm group includes banana trees, palms, rose bushes, maples, coffee bushes, tomato plants, cotton bushes, pumpkins, grapevines, rice, wheat, oats, and many other familiar plants.

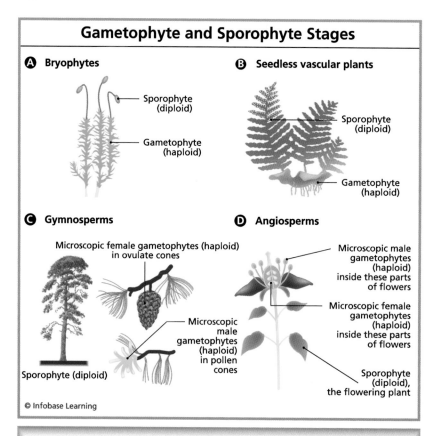

Gametophyte and Sporophyte Stages

Ⓐ Bryophytes

Sporophyte (diploid)

Gametophyte (haploid)

Ⓑ Seedless vascular plants

Sporophyte (diploid)

Gametophyte (haploid)

Ⓒ Gymnosperms

Microscopic female gametophytes (haploid) in ovulate cones

Microscopic male gametophytes (haploid) in pollen cones

Sporophyte (diploid)

Ⓓ Angiosperms

Microscopic male gametophytes (haploid) inside these parts of flowers

Microscopic female gametophytes (haploid) inside these parts of flowers

Sporophyte (diploid), the flowering plant

© Infobase Learning

Figure 5.3 Plants exhibit gametophyte and sporophyte stages. A) The gametophyte stage is dominant in bryophytes, and the sporophyte is dependent on the gametophyte for nourishment. B) The sporophyte stage is dominant in seedless vascular plants, and the gametophyte is free-living. C) In gymnosperms, the gametophyte is reduced and dependent on the sporophyte. D) In angiosperms, the gametophyte is also reduced and dependent on the sporophyte.

Flowering plants live in most land habitats, as well as in both fresh water and salt water. They represent more than 80% of the planet's green vegetation.

The flower of an angiosperm is composed of modified leaves that form structures required for sexual reproduction. The basic components of a flower are:

- Sepals that enclose a flower before it opens.

- Petals that are interior to sepals and often have vibrant colors.
- A carpel that contains an ovary, style, and stigma. An ovary, which contains at least one ovule, sits at the base of the carpel. The style connects the ovary to the stigma, which receives pollen.
- A stamen composed of an anther and a filament that attaches an anther to the flower. Pollen grains are produced in the anther.

Some flowers self-pollinate, meaning that, the flower's sperm cells fertilize the flower's egg cells. In cross-pollination, pollen from

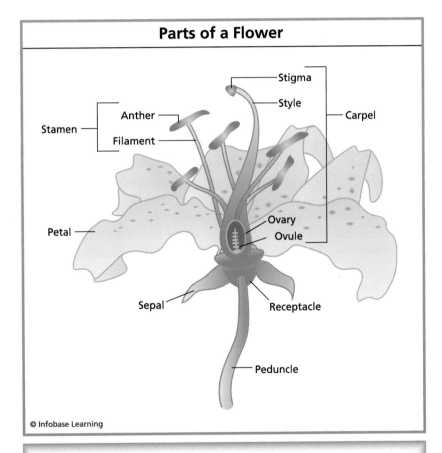

Parts of a Flower

© Infobase Learning

Figure 5.4 A typical flower consists of sepals, petals, stamens, and one or more carpels.

one plant travels to the stigma of a flower on another plant. For fertilization to occur, the pollen must reach a flower of the same species. Cross-pollination ensures genetic diversity within a species.

After fertilization, seeds develop from ovules. The wall of the ovary becomes thicker and matures into a fruit. Fruits protect seeds and help to disperse them. Some fruits are eaten by animals. Protected by their tough coat, seeds pass through an animal and are excreted

A Time for Reflection?

Humans continue to produce greenhouse gases that can increase global warming. Dr. Andy Ridgwell and his associates at the University of Bristol (United Kingdom) suggest that a careful selection of crops could reduce the warming trend. Crop plants generally have a higher solar reflectivity, or albedo, compared with natural vegetation and soil. By reflecting light, crop plants increase the amount of solar energy that returns to space. Certain crop varieties have a higher albedo due to the shininess and grouping of their leaves. As an example, sorghum varieties differ in albedo depending upon the presence or absence of an outer waxy coating.

Ridgwell says that a careful selection of food crops may cool Europe and North America up to 1.8°F (1°C) during the summer growing season. This would amount to a yearly global cooling of more than 0.18°F (0.10°C). The small amount of cooling may seem trivial. Yet it would represent about 20% of the temperature increase that the world has experienced since humans began massive creation of greenhouse gases during the Industrial Revolution.

Several approaches can be used to enhance solar reflectivity of crops. One way to increase albedo is to spray upper foliage with reflective substances, such as the mineral clay kaolinite. Scientists could selectively breed crop plants for increased reflectivity. Scientists could also alter the DNA of crop plants to increase leaf waxes and optimize leaf arrangements.

with fresh fertilizer. Yet not all fruits are meant to be eaten. To boost dispersal by winds, the fruits of dandelions have feathery tufts and those of maple trees have blades. Some fruits have barbs that attach to animal fur. The animal carries its passengers to new land.

PARTING WITH PLANTS

Seven hundred million years ago, algae thrived in the oceans. Some plants had adapted to life on land about 400 to 500 million years ago. Nonvascular plants developed tissues that protected gametes and embryos from drying in the open air. By 350 million years ago, some plants had vascular tissue that enhanced the uptake of water

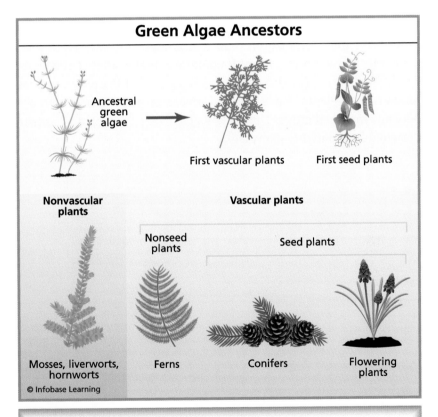

Figure 5.5 Fossil and biochemical evidence indicates that plants are descended from multicellular green algae.

and minerals from the ground, and increased the flow of sugars and other nutrients from photosynthetic leaves to the plant's body. Vascular tissue enabled plants to grow taller and successfully compete with nonvascular plants for sunlight. Around 360 million years ago, plants began to produce seeds, embryos stored with a food supply in a durable coat. The last major evolutionary change in plant life arrived around 140 million years ago: flowers that protect seeds and fruits that aid in seed dispersal. The angiosperms had arrived and began to dominate plant life.

More than 11,000 years ago, humans began to alter plants through agriculture. Farmers bred plants with preferred traits. In time, cultivated plants differed from species that grew in the wild. Take the maize plant, for example. Scientists propose that farmers first domesticated maize, or corn, in Mexico about 10,000 years ago. Maize was developed from the teosinte plant, a type of grass. Like maize, teosinte produces grains of starch. However, teosinte synthesizes much less starch than maize, and stores starch in seed pods only about 1.6 in. (4 cm) long, much smaller than a corn cob. Traditional agriculture breeding practices are not the only way that humans alter plants. Since the mid-1990s, farmers have grown genetically modified crops. These plants have new traits that scientists designed by modifying plant DNA.

Animals: From Sponges to Insects

Plants and animals share a common feature: Both types of life forms probably evolved from marine protists. Of course, plants and animals differ in many ways:

- Plant cells have cell walls and chloroplasts, and animal cells typically do not.
- Unlike plants, animal life cycles do not include haploid and diploid generations. Animals have diploid somatic cells and produce haploid gamete cells by meiosis.
- Plants are autotrophs that use sunlight for an energy source and carbon dioxide as a source of carbon. Animals are heterotrophs, and they rely upon organic carbon for their carbon source and source of energy.
- Plants extend their roots and stems in a search for nutrients. They do not have to move to eat. Most animals must move to find new sources of organic carbon, such as plants or animal prey.

An animal's diet of organic carbon can require a digestive system to break down food, muscles and a skeletal system to search for food, and a nervous system to coordinate muscles and to sense a new food supply. Animals need a way to distribute nutrients throughout the body, to deliver oxygen to cells, and to eliminate carbon dioxide and other waste products of cell activity. In short, animals need some form of circulatory system and respiratory system. The diversity among members of the animal kingdom reflects different solutions to the challenges of survival as heterotrophs.

Humans like to organize and classify things to simplify a complex world. For thousands of years, humans have devised schemes for classifying animals by their varied traits.

CLASSIFYING ANIMALS

Traditional methods of classifying animals focus on body shape and the development of embryos. Animals vary in body symmetry. Some animals have bodies with radial symmetry, in which body parts are arranged around a central axis. Each body part extends from the center of the animal. Identical halves can be produced if the animal were sliced along the central axis in more than one plane. Take a Styrofoam cup, for example. A cup can be cut in half—from top to bottom—in a number of places to produce identical halves. An animal that has radial symmetry has a top and a bottom, but lacks distinctive front and back sides, and left and right sides. Radially symmetrical animals tend to stay in one place. They allow food to come to them, rather than seek food.

Most animals have bodies with bilateral symmetry. Identical halves, or nearly identical halves, of such an animal can be produced only along a single plane. A human has bilateral symmetry that can be imagined as a line starting from the middle of the forehead and extending through the trunk to mark left and right halves. With their streamlined body shape, bilaterally symmetrical animals are more active than animals with radial symmetry. Animals with bilateral symmetry tend to move forward, and they have a head that contains sensory organs.

Animals are multicellular organisms. This means that activities required for survival and reproduction are performed by specialized groups of cells. The degree of cell organization varies among animals. Simpler types of animals have a cellular level of organization. Various activities are divided among cells, but cells performing similar activities are not arranged as functional units. A more complex level of cell organization is the tissue level of organization.

Radial vs. Bilateral Symmetry

Radial symmetry   Bilateral symmetry

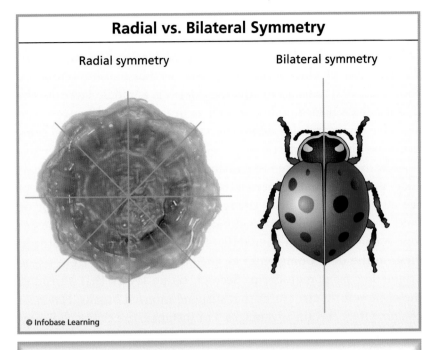

© Infobase Learning

Figure 6.1 This image shows the difference between an animal with radial symmetry, such as a jellyfish, and one with bilateral symmetry, such as a beetle.

Cells that perform similar or the same functions are grouped and perform their activities in a coordinated way. The liver, for instance, functions with groups of tissues. At the highest level of complexity, animals have an organ level of organization. Mammals, for example, have an immune system that is a group of organs working together to defend the body against foreign invaders and poisonous substances. Bone marrow, the spleen, tonsils, and other tissues play a role in the immune response. Most animals have at least a tissue level of organization, if not an organ system level of organization.

In animals with true tissues, the embryo develops layers of cells that form tissues and organs. The ectoderm layer covers the embryo's surface. The outer covering of an animal develops from this layer. In some animals, the central nervous system develops from the ectoderm layer. The innermost layer is the endoderm layer, which develops into the lining of the digestive tract. In some animals, the endoderm layer also develops into the liver and other organs. Animals that produce embryos with two tissue layers are called diploblastic. Many animals are triploblastic. The embryos of these animals produce three tissue layers as they mature: ectoderm, endoderm, and mesoderm. The mesoderm is a middle layer of cells that develops into muscles, as well as organs located between the digestive cavity and the outer covering. Animals with bilateral symmetry are also triploblastic.

Another feature used to classify animals is the absence or presence of a space that separates the digestive tract from the wall of the outer body. The body cavity, which may be filled with air or fluid, is called a coelom. Acoelomates are animals that lack a coelom. A coelomate is an animal that has a coelom with two features. First, in the developing embryo, the coelom develops from tissue originating from mesoderm. Second, tissue layers that surround the coelom form structures that suspend internal organs. Having a coelom offers certain advantages. For instance, the cavity allows an efficient circulatory system to deliver oxygen to cells and remove carbon dioxide and other wastes produced by cells. In contrast, acoelomates have a compact interior in which organs press upon one another and restrict movement of blood. Another advantage of a coelom is that it supports organs and allows the development of larger animals. A pseudocoelomate has a coelom formed from both mesoderm and endoderm. A pseudocoelom ("false coelom") lacks mesoderm on the inner side of the cavity. As a result, muscular or connective tissue does not develop to support the gut, and the size of the animal is limited.

Animals with bilateral symmetry are also grouped according to whether their embryos have a protostome or a deuterostome development. Several features distinguish protostomes and deuterostomes. The key feature concerns which end of an organism's digestive tract develops first: the front end or the rear end. As an embryo matures, an opening forms at one end of the embryo and develops into one end of the digestive tract. Later, another opening forms at the opposite end of the embryo, marking the other end of the digestive tract. In protostomes, the mouth develops from the first opening and the anus develops from the second opening. Deuterostomes develop an anus from the first opening and a mouth from the second opening.

In a traditional scheme, members of the animal kingdom are grouped by the following characteristics:

1. No true tissues
2. True tissues (Eumetazoa)
   a. Radial symmetry (Radiata) and diploblastic
   b. Bilateral symmetry (Bilateria) and triploblastic
      i. No body cavity (Acoelomates)
      ii. "False body cavity" (Psuedocoelomates)
      iii. Body cavity (Coelomates)
         1. Protostome development (Protostomia)
         2. Deuterostome development (Deuterostomia)

This method takes advantage of the body shape and development features previously discussed.

As scientists analyzed the genes of various animal species, the data suggested that animals with bilateral symmetry should be classified into the Deuterostomia, the Lophotrochoza, and the Ecdysozoa. An animal in the Lophotrochozoan group has one of two traits: a crown of tentacles called a lophophore that aids in feeding, or a stage in development known as trochophore larva. Animals in the Ecdysozoa group secrete an exoskeleton, a stiff covering for their bodies. As the animals mature, they undergo ecdysis. In this process, the animal sheds its old exoskeleton and secretes a new one to accommodate its larger body. This modified way to classify animals looks like this:

1. No true tissues
2. True tissues (Eumetazoa)
   a. Radial symmetry (Radiata) and diploblastic
   b. Bilateral symmetry (Bilateria) and triploblastic
      i. Protostome development (Protostomia)
         1. Crown of tentacles/trochophore larva (Lophotrochozoa)
         2. Shedding of exoskeleton (Ecdysozoa)
      ii. Deuterostome development (Deuterostomia)

It is time to place these classification terms in context with a brief survey of animals. The following section explores examples of animal types included in the categories of the modern classification scheme.

A SURVEY OF THE ANIMAL KINGDOM
Animals That Lack True Tissues

More than 8,000 living species of sponges are grouped into the Porifera. Most of these animals live in marine habitats. Sponges attach themselves to a surface, clinging to rocks and other animals. Some sponges have bodies with radial symmetry, while others are asymmetrical. The size of a sponge varies from about 0.08 inches (2 mm) to more than 6.6 feet (2 m). Sponges lack true tissues. A sponge does have collections of specialized cells loosely organized in a gelatinous matrix. A sponge is covered with cells that are like skin cells in other animals. Another type of cell, called a collar cell, lines the inside of the sponge. Amoeba-like cells scurry through the matrix, digesting food particles, and carrying nutrients to other cells. Sponges are filter feeders that gather particles of food by producing water currents with the beating flagella of collar cells. Water circulates through the sponge's porous body, carrying nutrients and oxygen. Water that leaves the body carries away wastes produced by cells.

A sponge can reproduce sexually or asexually. In sexual reproduction, sperm fertilize eggs in the central cavity of a sponge, and a fertilized egg forms a zygote that matures into a larva. Unlike an adult sponge, a sponge larva moves through water. When a young sponge matures into an adult, it basically becomes a couch potato of the sea, moving water to get its food. Sponges reproduce asexually by forming buds that detach from the parent sponge, float away, and develop into new sponges.

Animals with True Tissues and Radial Symmetry

The Cnidaria are one of the oldest groups of animals that have bodies with true tissues. They have a fossil history dating back more than 700 million years. The cnidarians include sea anemones, corals, Portuguese man-of-war, hydras, and jellyfishes. Like the sponges, the Cnidaria live in water and most live in saltwater. All cnidarians fit into one of two types: a polyp form and a medusa, or jellyfish, form. The polyp form is adapted for sedentary life, whereas the medusa form is adapted for floating. Polyps typically have tube-shaped bodies that attach to a surface. The medusa form can be imagined as a polyp in which the tubular part has been widened and flattened

Figure 6.2 Purple tube sponges, photographed in the Caribbean, are among the simplest animals on Earth. They may be used as shelter for invertebrates, such as crabs and shrimp.

into an umbrella shape. A medusa moves through water by drifting and by contracting its body. Some cnidarians, such as sea anemones and coral, exist only as polyps. Other cnidarians have life cycles with a polyp stage and a medusa stage. For example, certain jellyfish alternate between polyp and medusa stages in their life cycles, although the medusa stage dominates.

Cnidarians have radially symmetrical, sac-shaped bodies with a gastrovascular cavity located in the center of the body. A gastrovascular cavity has a single opening that serves as mouth and anus. The cavity functions in both digestion and circulation of nutrients. Like many simple types of animals, cnidarians lack a circulatory system to distribute nutrients throughout the body. Tentacles surround the opening into the gastrovascular cavity. The tentacles not only push prey into the cavity, but also contain cells that eject long threads to entangle prey, or barbed, stinging threads that may have

Figure 6.3 A Portuguese man-of-war, an animal made up of four separate polyps, feeds on fish. Its name comes from the uppermost polyp, a gas-filled bladder that sits above the water and resembles an old warship at full sail.

paralyzing toxins. Once food is inside the gastrovascular cavity, an inner layer of tissues secretes digestive juices. Food is digested and nutrients are circulated among cells within the cavity. The animals have muscle fibers and nerves that enable it to move in search of food. Cnidarians reproduce sexually, via fusion of sperm and egg cells, or asexually by budding.

Animals that Are Protostomes with Bilateral Symmetry

Animals that have a protostome development and bodies with bilateral symmetry can be divided into two groups: the Lophotrochozoan animals and the Ecdysozoa animals. Members of the lophotrochozoans include the Platyhelminthes (flatworms), Annelida, and the diverse group of mollusks.

Flatworms have the following features: acoelomate, triploblastic (i.e., ectoderm, mesoderm, and endoderm tissue layers), protostome development, an organ level of body organization, and bilateral symmetry. Flatworms are also interesting life forms that look like creatures from another planet. They have sac-like bodies with a single opening, muscles, a simple nervous system, and digestive organs. The animals lack any respiratory system to enable the uptake of oxygen from the environment and the elimination of carbon dioxide to the environment. However, flatworms live in water or in moist soil, and they are so thin that oxygen and carbon dioxide diffuse across the surface of their bodies.

Flatworms are divided into three groups: the planarians, the parasitic tapeworms, and parasitic flukes. The planarians and related flatworms live in freshwater. A typical planarian has an arrow-shaped head. The extension of the head on either side bears sensory organs to detect food or danger. Planarians look cross-eyed due to two light-sensitive spots on their head. The animals secrete mucous from their lower body that enables them to glide across a surface with their cilia. They also use their mucus to entangle prey. After wrapping itself around its food, a planarian extrudes an organ called a pharynx through its mouth. Although the pharynx is similar to a muscular throat, it is located around the middle of the planarian's body. The pharynx ejects digestive fluids on its food—living or dead—and sucks small pieces of partially digested food into a gastrovascular cavity for further digestion. Any undigested wastes leave the body

Figure 6.4 Planarians are unsegmented invertebrates. They have no specialized respiratory organs. Instead, oxygen and carbon dioxide diffuse across the surface of their flat bodies..

through the mouth. Planarians can reproduce sexually by producing both male and female gametes. A planarian reproduces asexually by constricting its body in half, separating into a head and a tail end. The two ends regenerate into whole planarians.

Two groups of flatworms are parasites. Tapeworms live inside the bodies of animals. While planarians have heads with sensory organs, the tapeworms do not. Instead, tapeworms have a front end with hooks and suckers used to attach to the intestinal wall of a host animal. The parasitic tapeworms also lack the nervous system and digestive system of planarians. Tapeworms absorb nutrients created by digestion processes in the host intestinal cells. Behind a short neck, a tapeworm consists of a strand of segments. Each segment contains a set of organs that produce male and female gametes. The gametes fertilize and eggs are formed. Tapeworm segments loaded with eggs exit the animal host in the feces, and await their own host animals. Humans can acquire tapeworms by eating improperly cooked meat from pigs or cows infected with the parasites.

Flukes are leaf-shaped parasites that live inside or outside animal bodies. Most adult flukes live inside a host body. The parasites have a poorly developed head with suckers that they use for attachment to a host. Like tapeworms, flukes have reduced nervous and digestive systems, but they have a highly effective reproductive system. Liver flukes and blood flukes inflict deadly illnesses in humans.

Members of the Annelida group are worms with bodies divided into similar segments. The familiar earthworm belongs to this group. Annelids have a true coelom, which contains more complex internal organs than those found in flatworms. Unlike the animals surveyed so far, annelids have a circulatory system with blood vessels to distribute nutrients and heart-like organs for pumping blood. Kidney-like nephridia organs remove wastes from the blood. Annelids also have a complete digestive system, and they have a nervous system that includes a brain. Some members of the group live in the sea, while others, such as earthworms, dwell in moist soil. An earthworm has tiny bristles on the outside of its body that anchor segments while the worm wriggles underground, literally eating its way through soil. As the soil passes through the worm's digestive system, it extracts nutrients. Although an earthworm produces both male and female gametes, two animals cross-fertilize by exchanging sperm. Some earthworms can reproduce by breaking off a section, which regenerates into an entire worm.

The Annelida group also includes leeches that have suckers at both ends. Leeches usually grow to lengths between 0.8 in. and 2.4 in. (2 cm to 6 cm). However, an Amazonian leech grows to about 12 in. (about 30 cm). Most leeches feed on fluids, and some feed on blood. Bloodsucking leeches use sharp jaws to slit the skin of an animal, or they gain access to blood by secreting enzymes to liquefy skin.

With the exception of the arthropods, the Mollusca group is the largest group of organisms alive today. Scientists have identi-fied more than 90,000 living species of mollusks. Most mollusks are marine animals, but some live on land or in freshwater. A mollusk body has two main parts: a soft visceral mass and a head-foot region. The visceral mass contains organs for digestion, reproduction, cir-culation, and respiration. The head-foot region contains organs for feeding and locomotion, as well as sensory organs. A muscular foot for movement or for attaching to a surface is one distinctive feature of mollusks. Two other mollusk traits are a radula and a mantle. A radula is a tongue-like organ bearing rows of teeth. Some radulas have as many as 250,000 tiny teeth. On the upper body, two folds of skin form a mantle that protects gills of some members. Most mol-lusks have a mantle that secretes a shell. The Gastropoda, Bivalvia, and Cephalopoda groups illustrate the diversity of mollusks:

- The Gastropoda group is the largest collection of mollusks and includes snails, land and sea slugs, sea butterflies, and sea hares. Many of the animals get their food by scraping plant material from surfaces with a radula. Some gastropods use their radula to drill into an animal for food.
- The Bivalvia group includes oysters, mussels, and clams. These animals have hinged, two-part shells secured by strong muscles. Bivalves lack a radula and a distinct head. Most of these animals sit in water and move cilia on the gills to create currents that carry food particles. When a foreign object, such as a grain of sand, becomes embedded between the shell and the mantle, the mantle secretes layers of a shiny material around the object. In this way, the animal produces a pearl.

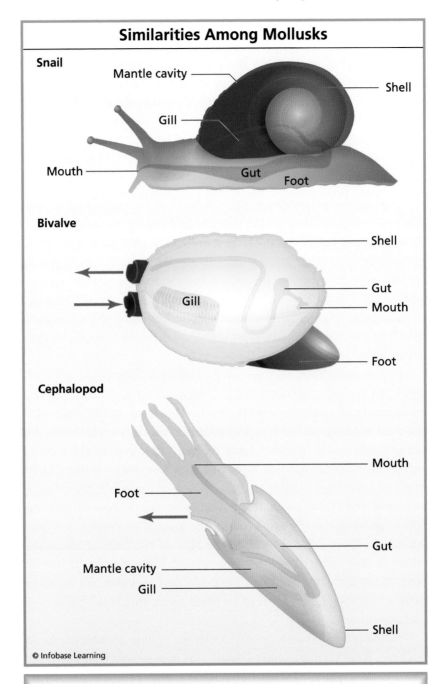

Figure 6.5 Three types of mollusks—snails, bivalves, and cephalopods—have some basic similarities.

- The Cephalopoda group includes octopuses, squids, and cuttlefish. Squids and octopuses propel themselves by squeezing water from their mantle cavity out through a modified foot that has a funnel shape. These animals use sucker-lined tentacles to hold prey and bring their food to their mouths. Cephalopods have a complex brain, a highly developed eye similar to that found in mammals, and they can learn. These traits support the cephalopod predatory lifestyle.

The second major group of animals that are protostomes with bilaterally symmetrical bodies are the Ecdysozoa animals. The Arthropoda group contains the largest collection of these organisms—more than 75% of all known animal species. Insects, crabs, mites, spiders, and many other life forms belong to this group. Arthropods are the most successful living animals on the planet and can be found thriving in most habitats. Depending upon the arthropod, they feed on other animals, plants, both plants and animals, or they live as parasites.

Arthropods have segmented bodies and segmented appendages. The typical arthropod body consists of a head, a thorax, and an abdomen. A cuticle covers the body. This hard, but flexible, exoskeleton is composed of layers of protein and chitin. The exoskeleton protects against physical hazards, helps to prevent dehydration, and an exoskeleton's inside layer provides a surface for the attachment of muscles. As they mature, young arthropods grow larger and must shed their protective covering by the process of molting. After shedding the old exoskeleton, the animal secretes a new one. An exoskeleton gains weight as the size of the animal increases, which is one factor that limits the size of arthropods that live on land. Many arthropods have a life cycle that includes the development of a young larval form to an adult form; this is the process of metamorphosis.

Arthropods have an open circulatory system in which a heart pushes a fluid through short vessels and into spaces that surround tissues and organs. Mollusks also have a type of open circulatory system. Arthropod respiratory systems are adapted to different lifestyles. Arthropods that live underwater have gills with thin layers of tissue that allow gas exchange. Land-dwelling arthropods have a network of air tubes that deliver oxygen to cells. Some arthropods have book lungs, a structure like a stack of plates, which allows the exchange of oxygen and carbon dioxide between air and a fluid that serves as the animal's blood. Arthropods have a nervous system with a brain. The head contains sensory organs, including compound eyes. Each compound eye has up to several thousand light detectors

Cephalopod Camouflage

"Cephalopods are the most changeable animal on earth for camouflage," said senior scientist and animal camouflage expert Roger Hanlon in a press release of the Marine Biological Laboratory (Woods Hole, Massachusetts). "There is no animal group that can equal it for speed or diversity of disguise. They have the widest range of patterns and they have the fastest change."

Fishes, insects, reptiles, and other animals use various tactics to blend into the background. For more than 35 years, Hanlon has studied the ways that animals disguise themselves. He discovered that animals use three camouflage methods. Squids, cuttlefishes, and octopuses use all three strategies for disguise. And the cephalopods can alter their appearance in milliseconds.

Two camouflage tactics, the uniform and mottled techniques, enable an animal to match its background. A uniform body pattern has little or no contrast; it lacks spots, stripes, and other patterns. A cephalopod uses a uniform body pattern when sitting on evenly colored sand or in shadows. A mottled pattern has light and dark patches distributed across the body. The colors of the patches match the colors of objects in the background. With disruptive coloration, an animal obscures its outline by displaying differently colored shapes. For example, squids produce slanting bars to break up the outline of their long bodies. Animals may use background matching and disruptive tactics in the same pattern. Humans combine the two methods in the design of fabric for military clothing.

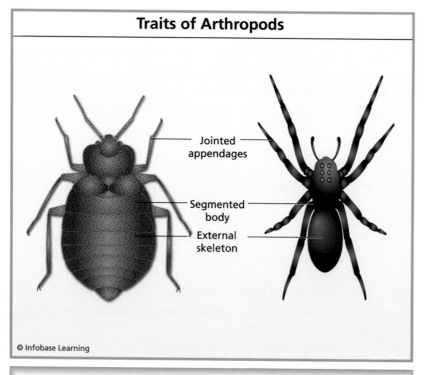

Traits of Arthropods

Jointed appendages

Segmented body

External skeleton

© Infobase Learning

Figure 6.6 All arthropods have jointed appendages, a segmented body, and an exoskeleton.

and lenses to focus light. Honey bees have more than six thousand light detectors and lenses per eye.

The arthropod group has been divided into many subgroups. Three of these are the cheliceriformes, the crustaceans, and the hexapods.

The cheliceriformes group includes ticks, spiders, mites, scorpions, sea spiders, and horseshoe crabs. These animals have a head and thorax fused into a segment called the cephalothorax. Six pairs of appendages are attached to the cephalothorax. The first pair of appendages is used as feeding organs; the second pair may be used for feeding, as sensory organs, or as pincers; and the remaining four pairs of appendages are walking legs. Most of these animals eat by sucking liquid from another animal. For example, spiders eject digestive enzymes onto prey and then use a strong pharynx to suck liquefied tissues.

The crustacean group includes animals that live in the sea and a few that live in freshwater. Examples of crustaceans are crabs, shrimp, lobsters, barnacles, and crayfish. Crustaceans typically have a distinct head, thorax, and abdomen. In addition, crustaceans have two pairs of antennae that serve as sensory organs, a pair of mandibles for chewing, two pairs of maxillae for handling food, and a pair of compound eyes. Crustaceans use appendages attached to their thorax and abdomen for swimming or walking.

The hexapoda group includes insects, the largest and most diverse group of arthropods. They differ from other arthropods because they have three pairs of legs and usually two pairs of wings on the thoracic body area. The wings are extensions of the cuticle, rather than modified appendages. Insects use a tracheal system to obtain oxygen and to get rid of waste carbon dioxide. The system is

Ancient Web Weavers

So far, the oldest fossils of spider-like animals date to about 380 million years ago. They were found in upstate New York. The extinct creatures could have been among the first land-dwelling animals in North America. *Attercopus fimbriunguis* differed from spiders that live today. Modern spiders weave their webs by ejecting silk strands from flexible spigots on modified appendages called spinnerets. The ancient creatures weaved wide sheets of silk from their spigots, which were fixed on plates attached to the animal's lower side. *A. fimbriunguis* did not have flexible spigots required to create webs. Scientists propose that the ancient creature used silk to make trails and to line burrows. *A. fimbriunguis* differed from modern spiders in another way: The extinct animal had a long, jointed tail. The tailed animals may have lived for 80 million years before the ancestors of modern spiders.

composed of a network of thin-walled tubes that reach every part of the body. The tubes open to the outside by spiracles. An insect usually has two pairs of spiracles on the thorax and seven or eight pairs on the abdomen.

The next major group of animals is characterized by bilateral symmetry and deuterostome development. This group includes whales, snakes, fish, sharks, kangaroos, frogs, tigers, monkeys, and humans.

Animals: From Sea Stars to Humans

Let us explore animals classified as Deuterostomes. The name of the group is unfamiliar to many. However, its members are very well known: fish, amphibians, reptiles, birds, and mammals.

THE THREE GROUPS OF DEUTEROSTOMES

Scientists have divided animals with deuterostome development among three groups: the Echinodermata, the Hemichordata, and the Chordata. Living members of the echinoderm group are inactive or slow-moving marine animals. The group includes sea stars (starfish), sea lilies, sea urchins, and sea cucumbers. Most echinoderms have larvae with bilaterally symmetrical bodies. As they mature, echinoderms lose their bilateral symmetry, transforming into a shape that almost has radial symmetry. Unlike typical radially symmetrical animals, adult echinoderms move to find food and shelter. Adult echinoderms have an endoskeleton made of spiny plates, but they lack a head and a brain.

The flattened body of sea stars consists of a central disk that extends into tapering arms. Sea stars usually have five arms, but some have multiples of five. A sea star's mouth is located on its lower side. The animal has spines that are extensions of its endoskeleton plates.

Figure 7.1 The underside of this brittle star shows its mouth. Also visible are numerous tube feet and a short, injured arm, which will grow back.

Sea stars perform gas exchange with gills, and they have a nervous system. Like other echinoderms, sea stars have an unusual feature. They use part of the coelom as a water vascular system that creates hydraulic power to operate extendable tube feet. The system is composed of a network of water-filled canals that branch into tube feet, which line grooves on the lower surface of a sea star's arms. The animal extends and contracts the feet by varying water pressure in the canals.

Sea stars like to eat bivalves. They move over their prey, position arms over each side of the hinged shell, and pry open the shell with their tube feet. Then, the sea star turns its stomach inside out and pushes it into the opening. The stomach secretes digestive enzymes that liquefy the bivalve's soft viscera. The sea star stomach takes in partially digested pieces for later digestion.

Sea stars reproduce both asexually and sexually. Some species of sea stars can reproduce asexually by regenerating a body from a detached arm that includes part of a central disk. Sexual reproduction is achieved with eggs and sperm produced by separate sexes.

The marine-dwelling acorn worms and sea angels are classified as Hemichordata. The animals have a nerve cord in the dorsal, or back, part of their bodies. The nerve cord is similar to the type of nerve cord found in animals of the Chordata group. An acorn worm has a soft, cylindrical, worm-shaped body divided into a proboscis, a collar region with a mouth, and a long trunk. The animal uses its proboscis to burrow into sand. Sticky mucus on the proboscis traps small organisms and other food particles, which are moved to the mouth with cilia. Acorn worms lack a respiratory system and perform gas exchange in the body surface and on gill slits.

The Chordata group has highly adaptable members that thrive in almost every habitat on the planet. At some point in its life cycle, a chordate displays the following traits:

- A hollow nerve cord located in the dorsal part of the animal. Pairs of nerves branch from the nerve cord and supply muscles. In many chordates, the front end of the nerve cord enlarges into a brain.
- A semi-flexible rod called a notochord, which is located just interior to the nerve cord, between the nerve cord and the digestive tract. The notochord extends through the length of the body.
- Gill slits that penetrate the throat, and play a role in gas exchange, feeding, or both functions.
- An organ in the throat called an endostyle. In some chordates, the endostyle secretes mucus to entangle small particles of food drawn into the throat by the action of cilia.

Most chordates also have an internal skeleton, the endoskeleton. An endoskeleton grows with a growing body and provides a structure that enables muscles to function. Chordates also typically have a tail that appears at least during embryonic development. Certain animals that are not chordates have an open circulatory system in which a bloodlike fluid travels through short vessels and into spaces that surround tissues and organs. Chordates have a closed circulatory system. Blood travels through vessels, but does not pour into open spaces. Some chordates also have a heart located in the front, or ventral, part of the body.

Certain chordates have an endoskeleton with a backbone composed of vertebrae, which typically enclose the dorsal nerve cord.

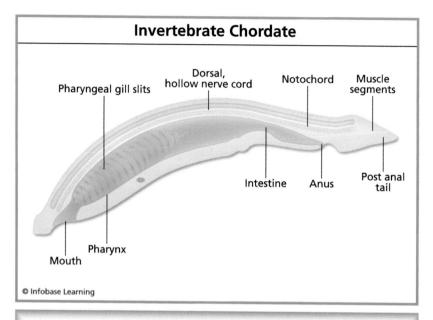

Invertebrate Chordate

© Infobase Learning

Figure 7.2 Chordates can be either vertebrates or one of closely related invertebrates. Yet, at some period in their life, every chordate will have certain specific traits.

These animals are the vertebrates, and they are one of the most diverse groups of life forms. Other chordates, the invertebrates, lack a vertebral column. Tunicates and lancelets are examples of invertebrate chordates. Both types of animals live in the sea. A familiar type of tunicate is the sea squirt.

The vertebrate group of chordates includes fish, amphibians, reptiles, birds, and mammals. In addition to vertebrae, vertebrates share a number of characteristics, including:

- Segmented muscles for highly controlled movement.
- A complete digestive tract.
- A closed circulatory system of arteries, veins, and capillaries.
- A ventral heart with chambers.
- An excretory system with paired kidneys.
- A brain consisting of three parts: forebrain, midbrain, and hindbrain.
- Paired sense organs.

Vertebrates also typically have a protective covering with an outer epidermis of epithelium and an inner dermis of connective tissue. Depending upon the animal, the endoskeleton may consist of bone or cartilage. The skeleton and muscles form a musculoskeletal system that enables a vertebrate to move quickly and efficiently.

SURVEY OF THE VERTEBRATES

Fish

The first vertebrates lived in the ocean and had traits in common with fish. They used gills for gas exchange and had small fins. Unlike most living fish, they lacked jaws, and probably obtained food by filtering water. Today, jawless lampreys and the hagfish resemble their extinct ancestors. The slender, eel-like fish scavenge for food or prey upon other fish. The jawless fish have medial fins, but they lack lateral fins. As a result, the jawless fish are not skilled swimmers and move by undulation.

Two types of fish have jaws: the cartilaginous fish and the bony fish. Cartilaginous fish have endoskeletons made of cartilage, a tough, elastic tissue. The animals have jaws, teeth, and both lateral and medial fins. They first appeared about 400 million years ago, and today, they are represented by sharks, rays, and skates. Since the animals are denser than water, they must swim or sink. They do rest on the ocean floor. Rays and skates have enlarged lateral fins that they flutter like wings as they glide through water. Sharks have dorsal (medial) fins, and paired pectoral and pelvic fins. The skin is covered with small, tooth-like scales. Although most sharks are predators, the largest shark—the whale shark—feeds by filtering small crustaceans from water. Shark egg cells are fertilized internally in females. Some sharks lay protected eggs that hatch outside the mother's body, while others release zygotes into water, and still other sharks retain zygotes until they mature into young sharks.

Bony fish live in the sea as well as freshwater. As their name indicates, these fish have an endoskeleton made of bone. Like the cartilaginous fish, bony fish have lateral and medial fins. Most of the bony fish also have a gas-filled sac—a swim bladder—that controls the animal's buoyancy and serves as a ballast tank. Bony fish can remain motionless in water simply by removing or adding air to the swim bladder. In contrast, a shark lacks a swim bladder and must swim to avoid sinking. This constant use of energy ensures that a shark has a healthy appetite. Most bony fish have skin covered with flat, bony scales. Bony fish have separate sexes and most reproduce by releasing gametes into the water. Sperm fertilize eggs, and the resulting zygote develops in water.

Scientists have divided the many types of bony fish into the lobe-finned fish and the ray-finned fish. Six species of lungfish and two species of coelacanth comprise the group of living lobe-finned fish. These fish have fins supported by rod-shaped bones wrapped in muscle that are similar to the leg and arm bones of land-dwelling animals. Lungfish typically live in swamps and stagnant ponds in Australia, Africa, and South America. They perform gas exchange with both gills and lungs (modified swim bladders), and they can live on land for extended periods of time. Until 1938, scientists thought that the ocean-dwelling coelacanths had been extinct for about 70 million years. Since then, several hundred coelacanths have been captured. A coelacanth's swim bladder is filled with oil and fat to increase buoyancy.

The group of ray-finned fish includes more than 23,000 species. Trout, sturgeons, gars, perch, salmon, and tuna are examples of ray-finned fish. The fish hold their fins away from their bodies with thin, ray-shaped bones. They survive by preying on insects and other small animals, or by filter feeding.

Amphibians and Reptiles

The group of amphibians includes toads, newts, frogs, and salamanders. Amphibians typically spend the early part of their lives in water, and then live on land as adults. Like fish, amphibians are ectothermic, or cold-blooded; the external temperature of the environment determines their body temperature. Ectotherms become sluggish in cooler temperatures and hibernate when temperatures turn too cold to sustain the animal's activities. Amphibians differ from fish in many ways. Amphibians have an endoskeleton of bone and cartilage, limbs adapted for walking on land, a larger brain, ears adapted for detecting sound transmitted through air, lungs for gas exchange in the adult, and smooth skin that plays a role in gas exchange. Most amphibians return to water to reproduce. Females deposit egg cells

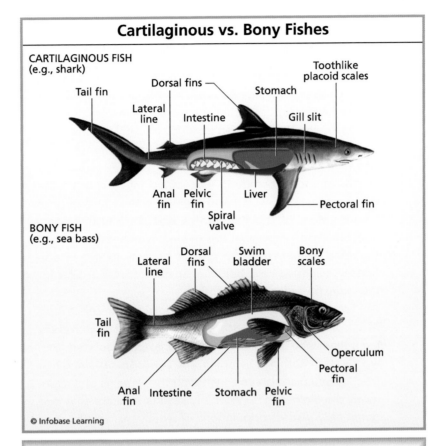

Cartilaginous vs. Bony Fishes

CARTILAGINOUS FISH
(e.g., shark)

Tail fin · Dorsal fins · Lateral line · Intestine · Stomach · Toothlike placoid scales · Gill slit

Anal fin · Pelvic fin · Spiral valve · Liver · Pectoral fin

BONY FISH
(e.g., sea bass)

Lateral line · Dorsal fins · Swim bladder · Bony scales

Tail fin

Anal fin · Intestine · Stomach · Pelvic fin · Operculum · Pectoral fin

© Infobase Learning

Figure 7.3 Cartilaginous fishes have skeletons made of flexible connective tissue called cartilage, rather than bone.

in water and males fertilize the eggs with sperm. The aquatic larvae that hatch from eggs have gills, which are lost as the animal develops into an adult that lives on land and breathes with lungs.

Alligators, crocodiles, snakes, turtles, and lizards are members of the reptile group. Most reptiles live in the tropics or subtropics. While some reptiles, such as snakes, live on land, other reptiles, such as alligators, spend most of their lives in water. Unlike amphibians, reptiles do not rely on water to reproduce. Fertilization occurs internally. In a further adaptation to living on land, many reptiles lay amniotic eggs that represent one of the most important differences between reptiles and amphibians. While amphibian eggs are coated

Unraveling Secrets in Mammoth DNA

At one time, elephant-sized mammoths shambled across every continent except Australia and South America. Scientists have proposed that ancestors of mammoths and the Asian elephant evolved in Africa about 7 million years ago. Around 5 to 6 million years ago, one mammoth species migrated to China, Siberia, and North America. The North American mammoth was joined much later by the woolly mammoth, which had crossed a land bridge from Siberia. Most of the mammoths had died 11,000 years ago. Small populations of the animals lived another several thousand years before the species became extinct. Traditionally, scientists have held human hunters responsible for the extinction of the mammoths.

To study the genetics of the woolly mammoth, Webb Miller and Stephan C. Schuster of Penn State University led a team who analyzed mitochondrial DNA isolated from woolly mammoth hair samples. The scientists obtained hair from museum specimens, including the remains of a mammoth discovered in 1799. Early results indicate that two genetically distinct populations of woolly mammoths lived at the same time. One Siberian population had died by 45,000 years ago. Since humans did not live in the region at the time, hunters could not have slaughtered the animals. The mammoths might have died from disease or due to climate change as Earth warmed.

In another study, the Penn State group tackled the mysteries of DNA isolated from nuclei of mammoth cells. They isolated DNA from two Siberian woolly mammoth mummies—one about 20,000 years old and the other at least 60,000 years old. By the time that they had analyzed half of the mammoth's genome, they confirmed that several species of woolly mammoth lived at the same time. Fossils did not hint at this possibility. Miller says that an understanding of the disappearance of the woolly mammoth and other animals may offer lessons about living animals that face extinction.

with a jellylike membrane, a protective shell covers the outside of a reptile's amniotic egg. The inside of the egg contains compartments with different functions that maintain the life of an embryo:

- The chorion is a hard covering that prevents the loss of water, while allowing the exchange of oxygen and carbon dioxide.
- The allantois serves as storage for waste products of cell activity.
- The fluid-filled sac of the amnion protects the embryo and prevents dehydration.
- The yolk sac contains nutrients for the embryo.

Some reptiles are viviparous and give birth to live young.

Reptiles have a tough, dry skin that contains keratin protein. The skin protects the animal from physical injury and prevents water loss. Reptiles have jaws and jaw muscles designed to hold and crush prey. The animals rely on their lungs for gas exchange and breathe differently than amphibians. Amphibians use their mouths to force air into the lungs. Reptiles use a more efficient method of drawing in air by expanding the chest cavity. Most reptiles have a three-chambered heart, whereas crocodile hearts have four chambers.

Birds

Birds resemble reptiles in many ways. In fact, they are more similar to reptiles than any other group in the animal kingdom. One difference between birds and reptiles is that birds are endothermic and maintain a body temperature around 104°F (40°C). An animal that is endothermic, or "warm-blooded," does not have to rely upon heat from the environment. This allows endothermic animals to live in habitats that are too cold for ectothermic animals. Feathers—the characteristic that distinguishes birds from any other animal alive today—create a layer of insulation that allows birds to retain body heat. Scientists propose that feathers, which are made of keratin, evolved from scales that cover the bodies of reptiles.

The ability to fly also distinguishes birds from reptiles. In addition to feathers, birds have many adaptations that enable flight, including a streamlined body, forelimbs reshaped as muscular wings, strong

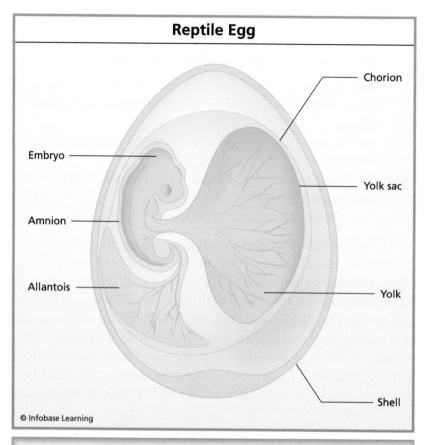

Reptile Egg

Chorion

Embryo

Yolk sac

Amnion

Allantois

Yolk

Shell

© Infobase Learning

Figure 7.4 A reptile's egg includes an amnion, which encloses the embryo in amniotic fluid for protection.

bones with air spaces and braces that replace heavy bone marrow tissue, lightweight beaks that lack teeth, excellent nerve and muscle coordination, and acute eyesight. Birds quickly and efficiently circulate oxygen to their cells with a powerful, four-chambered heart that pumps blood under high pressure. Among the vertebrates, the bird respiratory system has a unique feature that increases lung capacity: air sacs. A bird's lungs connect with about nine air sacs in the abdomen and thorax, which extend by small tubes into long bones. Air sacs improve the efficiency of the respiratory system and also serve as a cooling system. Not all birds fly; penguins swim, while emus and ostriches run.

Birds reproduce with internal fertilization and production of a hard-shelled egg. The embryo in the egg develops outside the female's body. Like reptiles, birds produce amniotic eggs. A difference between reptile and bird eggs is that bird eggs contain albumin, a protein component of egg white.

Mammals

Mammals occupy most habitats on the planet. They can be found living in the oceans and in freshwater, flying through the air, and on land from the tropics to the poles. Hair is one key feature that distinguishes mammals from other animals. Hair serves as an insulator that helps endothermic mammals control their body temperature. In different mammals, hair also provides camouflage, grows into spines for protection, and enhances the sense of touch in the form of whiskers. Mammals share many other unique traits including:

- Mammary glands that produce nutrient-rich milk for the young.
- Three inner ear bones that enable an acute sense of hearing.
- Efficient regulation of body temperature.
- Sweat glands to decrease body temperature.
- A layer of fat under the skin that provides additional insulation and a source of high-energy compounds.
- Convoluted bones in the nasal cavity that warm and moisten inhaled air and reduce moisture loss when exhaling.
- Large brain size.
- Specialized teeth for grinding, shearing, or cutting, which enable mammals to eat a variety of foods.
- A muscular diaphragm to increase air circulation of the lungs.

Mammals are divided among three groups: the monotremes, the placental mammals, and the marsupials. Scientists consider the monotremes—the duck-billed platypus and spiny anteater—to be the most primitive mammals. These stocky animals with squat legs and a short tail live in New Guinea and Australia, and produce eggs similar to bird eggs. A female platypus burrows into the ground to lay eggs, while the spiny anteater incubates eggs in a pouch. Unlike the mammary glands of other mammals, monotreme mammary glands lack nipples. A female secretes milk on her belly, and the young suck milk from the fur.

The placental mammals include cats, bats, mice, wolves, whales, tigers, dogs, horses, apes, and humans. Ninety-four percent of mammals are placental mammals, a group that is also known as the Eutherians. In a pregnant placental mammal, the lining of the mother's uterus and tissue from the embryo fuse to form a placenta. A placenta enables the exchange of oxygen, nutrients, and a fetus's waste products between maternal blood and fetal blood. Placental mammals tend to spend more time caring for their newborn, compared with other animals.

While many types of mammals are placental mammals, the primates merit a brief look. The primate group includes tarsiers, monkeys, lemurs, and the apes, a category that includes humans. Primates typically have flat nails instead of claws, and hands and feet ideal for grasping. While all primates have thumbs separate from the other fingers, monkeys and apes have fully opposable thumbs. Compared with other mammals, primates have short jaws and a large brain. Humans differ physically from living apes in many ways. For example, humans have reduced hair growth, walk on two legs, and stand upright. People also have a jawbone that is further reduced in size. A larger brain enables verbal communication more complex than the speech of other primates.

The group of marsupial mammals includes the kangaroo, opossum, and koala. Marsupials display yet another variation for sexual reproduction. After fertilization, a shell membrane forms around an embryo in the uterus. Several days later, the embryo breaks out of the shell and creates a depression in the wall of the uterus where the embryo absorbs nutrients with a simple type of placenta called a yolk sac placenta. While still in an embryonic stage of development, a young marsupial crawls out of the mother's uterus and continues development outside her body. In most marsupial species, the young animal nestles into the mother's pouch, and attaches to a teat as it continues to mature.

Marsupials once lived around the world. Today, marsupials live in the Australian region and in North and South America. North American marsupials are represented by a few species of opossum. In the ancient past, Australia was joined with South America in a

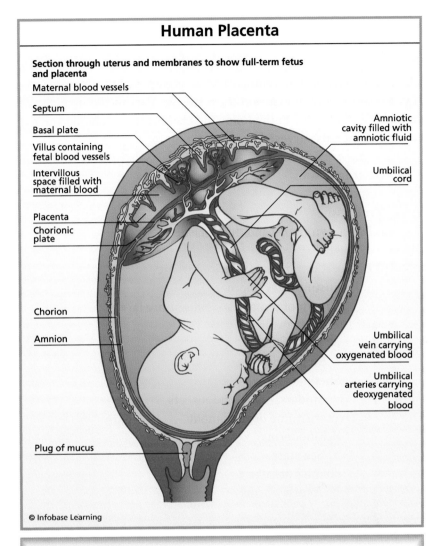

Human Placenta

Section through uterus and membranes to show full-term fetus and placenta

Maternal blood vessels

Septum

Basal plate

Villus containing fetal blood vessels

Intervillous space filled with maternal blood

Placenta
Chorionic plate

Chorion

Amnion

Plug of mucus

Amniotic cavity filled with amniotic fluid

Umbilical cord

Umbilical vein carrying oxygenated blood

Umbilical arteries carrying deoxygenated blood

© Infobase Learning

Figure 7.5   A human fetus has numerous support structures around it in the human body.

supercontinent called Pangaea. After the supercontinent broke apart, Australia experienced 65 million years of isolation. During this time, marsupials evolved into various animals similar to the many types of placental animals that evolved in other parts of the world. This type of evolution is called convergent evolution.

ADIOS TO THE ANIMALS

The previous two chapters explored the many ways that animals adapted to consuming organic carbon, as opposed to obtaining energy from the Sun and carbon from the air. Part of the diversity of animal life is reflected in the following classification scheme and examples of animals surveyed:

1. No true tissues
   a. Sponges
2. True tissues
   a. Radial symmetry and diploblastic
      i. Jellyfish
   b. Bilateral symmetry and triploblastic
      i. Protostome development
         1. Crown of tentacles/trochophore larva
            a. Flatworms
            b. Earthworms
            c. Snails, clams, and squids
         2. Shedding of exoskeleton
            a. Spiders, crabs, and insects
      ii. Deuterostome development
         1. Echinoderms
            a. Sea stars
         2. Hemichordates
            b. Acorn worms
         3. Chordates
            a. Invertebrate chordates
               i. Tunicates
            b. Vertebrate chordates
               i. Fish
               ii. Amphibians
               iii. Reptiles
               iv. Birds
               v. Mammals

From the top of the scheme to its bottom, animals vary from those composed of aggregations of cells to animals that have complex organ systems, from animals with radial symmetry to animals with bilateral symmetry and a head equipped with sensory organs, from

Two Huge Animals

Thanks to special effects, enormous snakes inhabit horror movies. Truth is often stranger than fiction. Scientists have discovered fossils of a snake that would make movie monsters flee in terror. The ancient snake weighed more than 2,500 pounds (1,134 kilograms) and was about 45 feet (13.7 meters) long, compared with today's record holders—anacondas and pythons—that stretch to about 21.3 feet (6.5 m). Jason Head of the University of Toronto (Ontario, Canada) and his colleagues named the snake *Titanoboa*. The animal lived 60 million years ago in northeastern Columbia. Although the snake probably spent most of its life in water, it could slither onto land to relax in sunlight. Dr. Head suggests that the animal might have had a diet of ancient crocodiles.

The existence of *Titanoboa* gives a clue about the temperature of Columbia around 60 million years ago. Unlike birds and mammals, snakes rely upon heat from the environment to sustain metabolism. Scientists calculate that a snake the size of *Titanoboa* would require a temperature of at least 86°F to 93°F (30°C–34°C). This estimate agrees with climate models of that time in which a warm Earth had high concentrations of atmospheric carbon dioxide.

The ancient Diprotodon holds the record as the world's largest marsupial. The animal looked like a hornless, hairy rhinoceros with strong claws on the front feet. Diprotodons stood 5.9 feet (1.8 m) tall, had a length reaching up to 11.5 feet (3.5 m), and weighed around 5,512 pounds (2,500 kilograms, or 2.5 tons). The plant-eating animals were the counterparts of the mammoth and mastodon, two placental plant eaters that once thrived in America and Eurasia. The Diprotodon lived in Australia about one million years ago and became extinct around 15,000 years ago.

animals that lack a skeleton to animals that have an exoskeleton or an endoskeleton, and from sedentary marine animals happy to grab food particles from water to humans who explore other planets.

8

Challenges for a Healthy Planet

The previous chapters explored a very small number of the species that humans have grouped into six kingdoms. To date, scientists have found and classified less than 10% of the different types of organisms that inhabit the planet. As researchers discover new life forms, the numbers of known, living species should increase. However, the numbers of known species alive today are also decreasing as species become extinct and vanish from Earth. In 2008, the International Union for Conservation of Nature and Natural Resources estimated that about 8,500 animal species and 8,400 plant species were threatened with extinction. More than 1,000 plant and animal species faced extinction in the United States alone.

LOSS OF SPECIES

Extinction is nothing new; it is a part of life. The fossil record of the last 200 million years indicates that species typically become extinct at a rate of one to two species a year. This seems to be a normal rate of species extinction. Earth also experiences abnormal rates of extinction. Huge numbers of species have become extinct at the same time during five mass extinctions. One mass extinction occurred about 240 million years ago. Within a few million years, about 96%

of marine animal species died out. Many land-dwelling species also became extinct. The fifth mass extinction took place about 65 million years ago, marking the end of more than half of all marine species and many species of land plants and animals, including dinosaurs.

Table 8.1 The Six Kingdoms			
Kingdom	General Traits	Number of Know Living Species	Examples
Eubacteria	Prokaryotic, unicellular	10,593	Mycoplasmas, cyanobacteria, spirochetes
Archaea	Prokaryotic, unicellular, differ chemically from Eubacteria species in rRNA, cell wall, cell membrane, and certain proteins	409	Methanogens, halophiles, thermophiles
Protists	Eukaryotic, unicellular	80,000	Amoebas, red algae, slime molds
Fungi	Eukaryotic, multicellular, heterotrophic, cell walls contain chitin	100,800	Mushrooms, mildews, yeasts
Plants	Eukaryotic, multicellular, autotrophic, cell walls contain cellulose	270,000	Mosses, ferns, redwoods
Animals	Eukaryotic, multicellular, heterotrophic, lack cell walls	1,320,000	Sponges, frogs, tigers

Sources: Kevin Kelly, "All Species Inventory." Whole Earth Magazine (Fall 2000): 4–10; Guillaume Lecointre and Hervé Le Guyader. The Tree of Life. Cambridge, Mass.: Harvard University Press, 2006.

Scientists warn that Earth may be heading toward a sixth mass extinction. Over the last 400 years, species have become extinct at a rate that may be 1,000 to 10,000 times faster than normal extinction rates. A new mass extinction would differ from earlier mass extinctions in a very important way. Scientists propose that natural disasters, such as asteroid strikes and excessive volcanic eruptions, have altered global climate, resulting in historic mass extinctions. Humans may be causing a sixth mass extinction. Human actions that increase the extinction of species include destruction of habitats, climate change, introduction of new species that affect native species, overexploitation of natural resources, spread of infectious diseases, and pollution.

Outcasts of the Six Kingdoms

The Six Kingdoms do not include certain entities that greatly affect living things: viruses, prions, and viroids. They are excluded because scientists do not consider them to be alive.

Viruses can be found around the globe—in water, in the ground, in the air, and frozen in polar ice. They infect protists, plants, animals, fungi, and bacteria. Viruses inflict human diseases on every continent. And yet, viruses consist of just two basic components: a DNA or RNA genome wrapped in proteins. Viral genomes are too small to encode all of the proteins required for reproduction. To reproduce, a virus infects a host cell. Viral genes force the cell to synthesize viral proteins and copies of the virus's genome, which assemble into viruses. New viruses can burst from a host cell with violence that kills the cell. Viruses that infect bacteria are called bacteriophages, or phages. The name *bacteriophage* means bacteria eater. Phages do not eat host bacterial cells. When it is time for new phages to depart from a host cell, they destroy it. In nature, phages play an important role in regulating the numbers of bacteria.

The loss of natural habitats may be the most important basis for a new mass extinction. Destruction of a habitat occurs when humans clear forests to plant crops or raise livestock, to make roads, or to expand cities. The United Nations and the Convention on Biological Diversity state that humans clear forests at a rate of 32 million acres (13 million hectares) each year. In the ancient past, forests and woodlands thrived on about half of the planet's land. So far, humans have reduced forest coverage to about 30% of Earth's land surface. Only about one-third of the remaining forests have not been significantly disturbed by human activity. When forests vanish, thousands of plant and animal species disappear as well. Humans are also altering freshwater

Prions are another exile from the kingdoms of life. All mammals have prion proteins in brain nerve cells. The prion proteins are called **Pr**ion **P**rotein-**C**ellular (PrPC). Normal PrPC proteins have a corkscrew shape. A cell usually eliminates any PrPC protein that flattens into an abnormal form of prion known as **Pr**ion **P**rotein-**Sc**rapie (PrPSc). When cells cannot get rid of mangled PrPSc proteins, the proteins form large masses, harm nerve cells, and injure the brain. Affected regions in a diseased brain become porous like a sponge. A person or animal with PrPSc proteins building up in nerve cells shows signs of brain damage. Disease-causing PrPSc proteins can spread like viruses. Examples of prion diseases include scrapie in sheep, mad cow disease, and Creutzfeldt-Jakob disease in humans. According to one theory, prion diseases spread because PrPSc proteins convert normal PrPC proteins into the abnormal PrPSc form. The new abnormal PrPSc proteins transform more normal PrPC proteins, and so on. The chain reaction spreads prion disease without the need for DNA or RNA.

The third exile is the viroid. Viroids are small RNA molecules that infect plants. Unlike viruses, viroids lack a capsid (protein shell surrounding its nucleus). These tiny RNA molecules cause at least 15 crop diseases that look like viral infections.

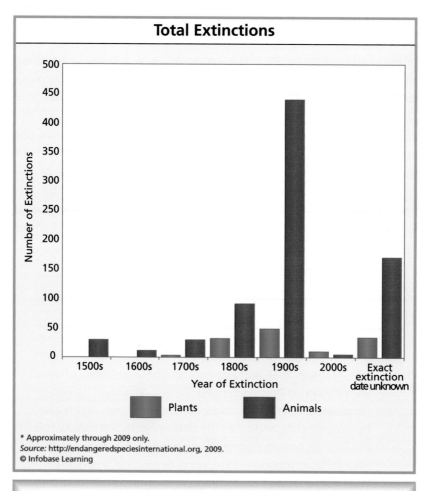

Total Extinctions

* Approximately through 2009 only.
Source: http://endangeredspeciesinternational.org, 2009.
© Infobase Learning

Figure 8.1 Animal and plant species continue to become extinct, and have been steadily reported and growing.

habitats by changing the course of rivers for hydropower and irrigation.

Many scientists argue that humans are changing global climate, which threatens the existence of species. Humans pour massive amounts of carbon dioxide into the air by burning fossil fuels. According to the European Commission, the executive body of the European Union (EU), levels of carbon dioxide have increased by 30% since the Industrial Revolution. Greater amounts of the greenhouse gas in the air raise the temperature of the planet and threaten many types of life forms. As one example, the U.S. Fish and Wildlife Service suggested that the polar bear should be listed as a threatened species. The main threat facing polar bears is the loss of ice due to global warming. Increased carbon dioxide in oceans also causes the water to become more acidic, which affects corals and animals that form shells.

Invasion of nonnative species is another important cause of species extinctions. Sometimes, the invasion occurs as a byproduct of human activity. Ships have carried rat stowaways to distant lands, for example. Humans have also intentionally delivered nonnative species to foreign lands. For instance, the Nile perch was introduced into Africa's Lake Victoria, and the new fish drove several native fish species to extinction. In some areas, native fish of commercial importance disappeared.

Overexploitation has caused the extinction of hundreds of species and threatens many more. Overexploitation occurs when people hunt, fish, or collect plants and animals at a rate that exceeds the ability of organisms to maintain their populations. Excessive fishing may pose the greatest threat to marine life.

Humans have accidently spread bacteria, viruses, and other organisms that cause infectious disease in plants and animals. One famous incident took place around 1826 when a whaling ship arrived in Hawaii. Sailors dumped water barrels infested with mosquito larvae. The larvae hatched, and the mosquito was introduced into a new land. The insect carried malaria—caused by a protozoan—and the pox virus to native birds, causing a major decline in bird populations.

Chemical pollution can threaten isolated populations of various organisms. For instance, nitrogen from crop fertilizer washes off soil, travels in rivers and streams, and out to sea. Excess nitrogen in sea water supports rapid growth of water-dwelling microscopic plants and algae. Following a growth spurt, the organisms die. Bacteria gorge on the dead plants and algae. As bacteria convert dead matter into useful molecules, they consume oxygen dissolved in water. The bacteria's feast depletes the water's oxygen content, making the water unfit for plants, crustaceans, fish, and other organisms. The result is a marine dead zone. One dead zone can be found at the mouth of the Mississippi River in the Gulf of Mexico. This dead zone can cover as much as 6,000 to 7,000 square miles (about 1,554,000–1,813,000 hectares).

Loss of habitat, invasion by nonnative species, and other factors do not occur in isolation. Many factors can combine to threaten living things. Consider the plight of amphibians. At least a third of the world's amphibians face extinction due to a mixture of threats, including:

- **Loss of habitat:** Amphibians lose habitats when humans divert streams, build dams, and drain swamps.
- **Pollution:** Amphibians exchange water and oxygen through their skin. Chemicals also seep through skin, increasing risk to disease and parasites, and inflicting deformities during early development.
- **Overexploitation:** While the pet industry has received its share of blame, a new type of overexploitation made the news in 2009. Human consumption of frog legs in Europe and Asia pose a serious threat to the survival of frogs.
- **Invasive species:** As one example, giant Central American cane toads were introduced in Australia during the 1930s to prey on insects that fed on sugar cane crops. The toads invaded native species' habitats.
- **Disease:** A lethal skin fungus has been killing amphibians across the globe.
- **Climate change:** Global warming may be increasing the growth of the deadly fungus that kills amphibians.

BIODIVERSITY

If the rate of species extinction exceeds the rate of new species formation, the planet loses biological diversity, or **biodiversity**. Biodiversity is a concept that refers to the variety and abundance of living things on Earth. Scientists also use the term to describe the variety of genes and traits within a species, as well as the collection of species in ecosystems. An ecosystem is a community of living creatures that interact with each other, and the soil, water, and air of the place where they live. Humans depend upon interactions within an ecosystem and interactions between ecosystems to provide necessities

Nutrient Flow in a Coastal Zone

Energy: sunlight

Plantlike protists

Nutrients rise

Dead matter settles to the bottom

Fungi and bacteria decompose dead matter

Filter feeders: clams, worms

© Infobase Learning

Figure 8.2 In a coastal zone, nutrients come from various sources for different creatures. As is true in any setting, the sun is the key factor in the flow of nutrients and continuation of life.

of life. As one example, interactions between the atmosphere and organisms in oceans and forests balance the amount of carbon available to form basic molecules of living things.

The planet's biodiversity supports human life in many ways, such as the provision of food. Humans depend upon plants as primary producers of nutrition. Over thousands of years, farmers cultivated food crops from plants that grew in the wild. Today, wild relatives of food crop plants play a vital role in food production. They are a source of genes that have been bred out of food crops. Scientists have used wild relatives of crop plants to improve the nutritional value of crops and to enhance resistance to disease. Successful crop production relies on many other types of organisms. Earthworms aerate soil, bacteria and fungi enrich soil, and insects pollinate plants. Amphibians, bats, and birds eat many types of insects that destroy plant crops.

Biodiversity has improved human health. For thousands of years, healers have used extracts of plants and animals to treat illnesses. Traditional medicine is still practiced in many parts of the world. Manufactured drugs also owe a debt to biodiversity. Drug stores sell

The Seed Vault

Many countries maintain seed banks to safeguard seeds of valuable crops. The seeds may be needed if a natural disaster or disease exterminates crop plants. If something destroys these seed banks, all may not be lost thanks to the Global Seed Vault, the ultimate backup for the seed banks. The Norwegian government built the vault deep inside a mountain on the Norwegian island of Spitsbergen, about 620 miles (1,000 kilometers) from the North Pole. A steel-and-concrete-lined tunnel leads to the vaults that can store up to 4.5 million seed samples. Each sample contains about 500 seeds. The vault should endure global warming and earthquakes. If the cooling system breaks down, Arctic temperatures outside the vault should preserve the seeds. Across the globe, plant breeders and farmers are planting seeds of endangered species. After the plants have produced seeds, portions of harvested seeds are sent to the underground vault for safekeeping. The facility opened on February 26, 2008, and within a year, the vault held more than 300,000 seed samples.

Figure 8.3 At the Svalbard Global Seed Vault on the Norwegian Island of Spitsbergen, packets of plant seeds are stored in boxes and packed in an underground vault. The seeds are duplicate samples of seeds held in seed banks around the world.

medicines that began as discoveries of the effects of plant and animal extracts. Examples of such drugs include:

- Taxol isolated from yew trees to treat cancer.
- Digitalin from the fox glove plant to treat heart problems.
- Quinine from the bark of cinchona trees to treat malaria.
- Pilocarpine from leaves of the plant *Pilocarpus jaborandi* to treat an eye disorder.
- A leech saliva protein to prevent blood clotting.
- Many antibiotics isolated from molds and bacteria.

According to the Biodiversity Project (Chicago, Illinois), about 20% of prescription drugs in the United States are derived from plants. The vast majority of plant species that grow in the disappearing tropical rain forests have not yet been tested for possible medical treatments.

Many governments sponsor projects to protect biodiversity. These efforts range from developing alternative fuels that would produce less greenhouse gas, decreasing the destruction of forests, stopping the flow of chemical pollutants into the environment, and protecting species in imminent danger of extinction. Awareness of the threat to biodiversity brings a new importance to the ancient practice of classification. Around the globe, scientists search for new species as part of the effort to conserve nature. Their goal is nothing less than to inventory the species diversity of the planet.

Glossary

autotroph   A type of organism that synthesizes nutrients from inorganic molecules and does not need to digest food to survive

base   A molecule that forms part of DNA and RNA

biodiversity   The variety and abundance of living organisms

chloroplast   Organelle that uses solar energy to produce complex sugar molecules, high-energy chemicals, and oxygen from water and carbon dioxide

chromatin   A mixture of proteins, DNA, and RNA

chromosome   A structure in a cell that contains DNA

cytoplasm   A gel-like matrix that fills the interior of a cell

deoxyribonucleic acid (DNA)   A nucleic acid molecule that encodes genetic information passed from one generation to the next

diploid   A cell with two matched sets of chromosomes in its nucleus

ecosystem   An area characterized by interactions between organisms in a particular habitat and between organisms and the physical environment of the habitat

endosymbiont   An organism that lives within the cell of another organism

eukaryote   A life form composed of one or more cells, in which the cells contain nuclei

gamete   An egg cell or a sperm cell

gene   A nucleotide sequence that encodes a protein or a functional RNA molecule

genome   The complete genetic information of an individual or species

habitat   The environment in which an organism lives

haploid   A cell with a single set of unmatched chromosomes in its nucleus

heterotroph   A type of organism that gets nutrients by digesting food

meiosis   A type of cell division required to produce egg cells and sperm cells

messenger RNA   An RNA molecule that transmits genetic information from DNA to a cell's protein-making apparatus

mitochondria   Organelles that function as a cell's power plant

mitosis   A type of cell division that produces two identical daughter cells

nucleus   The organelle that contains most of a cell's DNA

parasite   An organism that lives in or on another organism, which is harmed by the relationship

plasma membrane   A membrane that surrounds a cell

prokaryote   A single-celled organism that lacks a nucleus

ribonucleic acid (RNA)   A nucleic acid molecule composed of nucleotides that have four types of bases: adenine, cytosine, guanine, and uracil

somatic cell   A cell other than an egg cell or a sperm cell

species   The lowest rank of a classification system, which contains members that closely resemble one another

symbiont   An organism that forms a relationship with an organism of another species, in which the relationship benefits at least one organism

Bibliography

"Antonie van Leeuwenhoek (1632–1723)." BBC Web site. Available online. URL: http://www.bbc.co.uk/history/historic_figures/van_leeuwenhoek. shtml.

"Archaea, the Bug Next Door?" *Astrobiology Magazine* Web Site. Available online. URL: http://www.astrobio.net.

Bardell, D. "The Roles of the Sense of Taste and Clean Teeth in the Discovery of Bacteria by Antoni van Leeuwenhoek." *Microbiology Reviews* 47 (1982): 121–126.

Barel, C. D. N., R. Dorit, P. H., Greenwood, G. Fryer, N. Hughes, P. B. N. Jackson, H. Kawanabe, et al. "Destruction of Fisheries in Africa's Lakes." *Nature* 315 (1985): 19–20.

Barton, Nicholas H., Derek E. G. Briggs, Jonathan A. Eisen, David B. Goldstein, and Nipam H. Patel. *Evolution.* Cold Spring Harbor, NY: Cold Spring Harbor Laboratory Press, 2007.

Bates, Lucy A., Katito N. Sayialel, Norah W. Njiraini, Cynthia J. Moss, Joyce H. Poole, and Richard W. Byrne. "Elephants Classify Human Ethnic Groups by Odor and Garment Color." *Current Biology* 17 (2007): 1938–1942.

Brown, James R., and W. Ford Doolittle. "*Archaea* and the Prokaryote-to-Eukaryote Transition." *Microbiology and Molecular Biology Reviews* 61 (1997): 456–502.

Campbell, Neil A., Jane B. Reece, Lisa A. Urry, Michael L. Cain, Steven A. Wasserman, Peter V. Minorsky, and Robert B. Jackson. *Biology, Eighth Edition.* San Francisco: Pearson/Benjamin Cummings, 2008.

Cann, Alan J. *Principles of Molecular Virology, Fourth Edition.* New York: Academic Press, Inc., 2005.

Carter, John, and Venetia Saunders. *Virology: Principles and Applications.* West Sussex, England: John Wiley & Sons Ltd., 2007.

Chivian, Eric, and Aaron Bernstein (eds.). *Sustaining Life: How Human Health Depends on Biodiversity*. New York: Oxford University Press, 2008.

Comis, Don. "Plants Text Message Farmers When Thirsty." U.S. Department of Agriculture Web site. Available online. URL: http://www.ars.usda.gov/IS/pr/2008/080429.htm.

Debruyne, Regis, Genevieve Chu, Christine E. King, Kirsti Bos, Melanie Kuch, Carsten Schwarz, Paul Szpak, et al. "Out of America: Ancient DNA Evidence for a New World Origin of Late Quaternary Woolly Mammoths." *Current Biology* 18 (2008): 1320–1326.

DeLong, Edward F. "Oceans of *Archaea*." *ASM News* 69 (2003): 503–511.

Drews, Gerhart. "Ferdinand Cohn, a Founder of Modern Microbiology." *ASM News* (August 1999). Available online. URL: http://www.asm.org/Articles/Ferdinand.html.

Drews, Gerhart. "The Roots of Microbiology and the Influence of Ferdinand Cohn on Microbiology of the 19th Century." *FEMS Microbiology Reviews* 24 (2000): 225–249.

"Fungus Does the Dirty Work." *Breakthroughs Magazine* (Winter 1999-2000). Available online. URL: http://www.pnl.gov/breakthroughs/issues/1999-issues/winter/.

Gilbert, M. Thomas P., Daniela I. Drautz, Arthur M. Lesk, Simon Y. W. Ho, Ji Qi, Aakrosh Ratan, Chih-Hao Hsu, et al. "Intraspecific Phylogenetic Analysis of Siberian Woolly Mammoths Using Complete Mitochondrial Genomes." *Proceedings of the National Academy of Sciences USA* 105 (2008): 8327–8332.

Global Environment Outlook: Environment for Development (GEO-4) (2007). United Nations Environment Programme Web site. Available online. URL: http://www.unep.org.

Hanlon, R. T., C.-C. Chiao, L. M. Mäthger, A. Barbosa, K. C. Buresch, and C. Chubb. "Cephalopod Dynamic Camouflage: Bridging the Continuum between Background Matching and Disruptive Coloration." *Philosophical Transactions of the Royal Society B* 364 (2009): 429–437.

Hartwell, Leland H., Leroy Hood, Michael L. Goldberg, Ann E. Reynolds, Lee M. Silver, and Ruth C. Veres. *Genetics: From Genes to Genomes, Third Edition*. New York: McGraw-Hill, 2008.

Head, Jason J., Jonathan I. Bloch, Alexander K. Hastings, Jason R. Bourque, Edwin A. Cadena, Fabiany A. Herrera, P. David Polly, et al. "Giant Boid Snake from the Palaeocene Neotropics Reveals Hotter Past Equatorial Temperatures." *Nature* 457 (2008): 715–717.

Hickman, Cleveland P. Jr., Larry S. Roberts, Allan Larson, Helen L'Anson, and David J. Eisenhour. *Integrated Principles of Zoology, Thirteenth Edition.* New York: McGraw-Hill, 2006.

Horner-Devine, M. Claire, Karen M. Carney, and Brendan J. M. Bohannan. "An Ecological Perspective on Bacterial Biodiversity." *Proceedings of the Royal Society London – Series B* 271 (2004): 113–122.

Kelly, Kevin. "All Species Inventory." *Whole Earth Magazine* (Fall 2000): 4–8.

Koskinen, Perttu E. P., Chyi-How Lay, Steinar R. Beck, Katariina E. S. Tolvanen, Anna H. Kaksonen, Jóhann Örlygsson, Chiu-Yue Lin et al. "Bioprospecting Thermophilic Microorganisms from Icelandic Hot Springs for Hydrogen and Ethanol Production." *Energy & Fuels* 22 (2008): 134–140.

"Last Chance." *Science Illustrated* (September/October 2008): 60–67.

Lawton, Graham. "Uprooting Darwin's Tree." *New Scientist* 201 (2009): 34–39.

Lecointre, Guillaume, and Hervé Le Guyader. *The Tree of Life.* Cambridge, Mass.: Harvard University Press, 2006.

Loh, Jonathan (ed.). *2010 and Beyond: Rising to the Biodiversity Challenge.* Gland, Switzerland: World Wide Fund for Nature, 2008.

Ly, Kiet A., Christine A. Riedy, Peter Milgrom, Marilynn Rothen, Marilyn C. Roberts, and Lingmei Zhou. "Xylitol Gummy Bears Snacks: A School-based Randomized Clinical Trial." *BMC Oral Health* (July 2008). Available online. URL: http://www.biomedcentral.com/1472-6831/8/20.

Madigan, Michael T., and Barry L. Marrs. "Extremophiles." *Scientific American* 276 (1997): 82–87.

Margulis, Lynn, and Karlene V. Schwartz. *Five Kingdoms: An Illustrated Guide to the Phyla of Life on Earth, Third Edition.* New York: W. H. Freeman and Company, 1998.

Marsili, Enrico, Daniel B. Baron, Indraneel D. Shikhare, Dan Coursolle, Jeffrey A. Gralnick, and Daniel R. Bond. "*Shewanella* Secretes Flavins That Mediate Extracellular Electron Transfer." *Proceedings of the National Academy of Sciences USA* 105 (2008): 3968–3973.

Matz, Mikhail V., Tamara M. Frank, N. Justin Marshall, Edith A. Widder, and Sönke Johnsen. "Giant Deep-Sea Protist Produces Bilaterian-like Traces." *Current Biology* 18 (2008): 1–6.

Milius, Susan. "Mammals Encounter Tougher Times, New Assessment of Species Shows." *Science News* 174 (2008): 15.

Olsen, Gary J., and Carl R. Woese. "Archaeal Genomics: An Overview." *Cell* 89 (1997): 991–994.

Pennisi, Elizabeth. "A Mouthful of Microbes." *Science* 307 (2005): 1899–1901.

Parniske, Martin. "Arbuscular Mycorrhiza: The Mother of Plant Root Endosymbioses." *Nature Reviews Microbiology* 6 (2008): 763–775.

Pikuta, Elena V., Richard B. Hoover, and Jane Tang. "Microbial Extremophiles at the Limits of Life." *Critical Reviews in Microbiology* 33 (2007): 183–209.

Poulsen, Michael, and Jacobus J. Boomsma. "Mutualistic Fungi Control Crop Diversity in Fungus-Growing Ants." *Science* 307 (2005): 741–744.

Price, Gilbert J. "Taxonomy and Palaeobiology of the Largest-ever Marsupial, *Diprotodon* Owen, 1838 (Diprotodontidae, Marsupialia)." *Zoological Journal of the Linnean Society* 153 (2008): 369–417.

Rabeling, Christian, Jeremy M. Brown, and Manfred Verhaagh. "Newly Discovered Sister Lineage Sheds Light on Early Ant Evolution." *Proceedings of the National Academy of Sciences USA* 105 (2008): 14913–14917.

Rabosky, Daniel L., and Ulf Sorhannus. "Diversity Dynamics of Marine Planktonic Diatoms Across the Cenozoic." *Nature* 457 (2009): 183–187.

Ridgwell, Andy, Joy S. Singarayer, Alistair M. Hetherington, and Paul J. Valdes. "Tackling Regional Climate Change by Leaf Albedo Bio-Geoengineering." *Current Biology* 19 (2009): 146–150.

Ringeisen, Bradley R., Emily Henderson, Peter K. Wu, Jeremy Pietron, Ricky Ray, Brenda Little, Justin C. Biffinger, et al. "High Power Density from a Miniature Microbial Fuel Cell Using *Shewanella oneidensis* DSP10." *Environmental Science & Technology* 40 (2006): 2629–2634.

Rittmann, Bruce R., Rosa Krajmalnik-Brown, and Rolf U. Halden. "Pre-genomic, Genomic and Post-Genomic Study of Microbial Communities Involved in Bioenergy." *Nature Reviews Microbiology* 6 (2008): 604–612.

Schultz, Ted R., and Seán G. Brady, "Major Evolutionary Transitions in Ant Agriculture." *Proceedings of the National Academy of Sciences USA* 105 (2008): 5435–5440.

Secretariat of the Convention on Biological Diversity. *Global Biodiversity Outlook 2* (2006). Available online. URL: http://www.biodiv.org/GBO2.

Selden, Paul A., William A. Shear, and Mark D. Sutton. "Fossil Evidence for the Origin of Spider Spinnerets, and a Proposed Arachnid Order." *Proceedings of the National Academy of Sciences USA* 105 (2008): 20781–20785.

Shear, William A., Jacqueline M. Palmer, Jonathan A. Coddington, and Patricia M. Bonamo. "A Devonian Spinneret: Early Evidence of Spiders and Silk Use." *Science* 246 (1989): 479–481.

Soyer-Gobillard, Marie-Odile. "Edouard Chatton (1883–1947) and the Dinoflagellate Protists: Concepts and Models." *International Microbiology* 9 (2006): 173–177.

Stamets, Paul. "Earth's Natural Internet." *Whole Earth Catalogue* (Fall 1999): 74–77.

Steenhuysen, Julie. "Massive Effort Underway to Save Endangered Seeds." Reuters News Service. Available online. URL: http://www.reuters.com.

Stewart, Melissa. *Classification of Life*. Minneapolis: Twenty-First Century Books, 2008.

Thomas, Susan. "Mushrooms: Higher Macrofungi to Clean Up the Environment." Available online. URL: http://www.battelle.org/Environment/publications/EnvUpdates/Fall00/article4.html.

Venkataraman, Bina. "Ocean 'Dead Zones' on the Rise." *The New York Times*, August 15, 2008.

Vilà, Carles, Peter Savolainen, Jesús E. Maldonado, Isabel R. Amorim, John E. Rice, Rodney L. Honeycutt, Keith A. Crandall, et al. "Multiple and Ancient Origins of the Domestic Dog." *Science* 276 (1997): 1687–1689.

Walther, Zenta, and John L. Hall. "The Uni Chromosome of *Chlamydomonas*: Histone Genes and Nucleosome Structure." *Nucleic Acids Research* 23 (1995): 3756–3763.

Woese, Carl R., Otto Kandler, and Mark L. Wheelis. "Towards a Natural System of Organisms: Proposal for the Domains Archaea, Bacteria, and Eucarya." *Proceedings of the National Academy of Sciences USA* 87 (1990): 4576–4579.

Wong, Kate. "Decoding the Mammoth." *Scientific American* 300 (2009): 26–27.

Yovel, Yossi, Matthias Otto Franz, Peter Stilz, and Hans-Ulrich Schnitzler. "Plant Classification from Bat-Like Echolocation Signals." *PLoS Computational Biology* 4(3) (2008): e1000032.

Further Resources

Books

Blaxland, Beth. *Cephalopod*. New York: Chelsea House Publishers, 2002.

Diagram Group. *Biology*. New York: Chelsea House Publishers, 2006.

DiConsiglio, John. *There's a Fungus Among Us!* Danbury, Conn.: Children's Press, 2007.

Eamer, Claire. *Super Crocs and Monster Wings: Modern Animals' Ancient Past*. Toronto, Ontario. Annick Press, 2008.

Gibson, J. Phil and Terri R. Gibson. *Plant Ecology*. New York: Chelsea House Publishers, 2006.

Holmes, Thom. *Early Life*. New York: Chelsea House Publishers, 2008.

Rainis, Kenneth G. and Bruce J. Russell. *Guide to Microlife*. Danbury, Conn.: Children's Press, 1996.

Rodriguez, Ana Maria. *Secret of the Plant-killing Ants and More!* Berkeley Heights, N.J.: Enslow Publishers, Inc., 2008.

Tilden, Thomasine E. Lewis. *Belly-Busting Worm Invasions!* Danbury, Conn.: Children's Press, 2007.

Walker, Richard. *Genes and DNA*. New York: Houghton Mifflin Company, 2003.

Web Sites

Science Daily

http://www.sciencedaily.com/

The Science Daily Web site is a comprehensive source for news about science research, new species, and endangered species.

Encyclopedia of Life

http://www.eol.org/index

The staff at the Encyclopedia of Life Web site aim to provide information about all life on Earth. In the meantime, the Web site provides data on many species of plants, animals, and other organisms.

Todar's Online Textbook of Bacteriology
http://www.textbookofbacteriology.net/
> *The University of Wisconsin's Dr. Kenneth Todar offers a comprehensive resource for information about bacteria.*

Endangered Species Program
http://www.fws.gov/endangered/
> *This Web site of the U.S. Fish and Wildlife Service provides information and news about endangered species. Visitors can also read about endangered species and efforts to save them in the Endangered Species Bulletin.*

Tree of Life Web Project
http://tolweb.org/tree
> *The Tree of Life Web Project offers information about the many types of species that live on Earth, as well their evolutionary history.*

History of Life Through Time
http://www.ucmp.berkeley.edu/exhibits/historyoflife.php
> *This project of the University of California's Museum of Paleontology surveys biodiversity over time. Insights about evolution and methods of classification can be found here.*

Picture Credits

Index

Page numbers in *italics* indicate photos or illustrations; page numbers followed by *t* indicate tables or charts.

About the Author

Phill Jones earned a Ph.D. in physiology/pharmacology from the University of California, San Diego. After completing postdoctoral training at Stanford University School of Medicine, he joined the Department of Biochemistry at the University of Kentucky Medical Center as an assistant professor. Here, he taught topics in molecular biology and medicine, and researched aspects of gene expression. He later earned a JD at the University of Kentucky College of Law and worked for 10 years as a patent attorney, specializing in biological, chemical, and medical inventions. Dr. Jones is now a full-time writer. His articles have appeared in *Today's Science on File, The World Almanac and Book of Facts, History Magazine, Forensic Magazine, Genomics and Proteomics Magazine, Encyclopedia of Forensic Science, The Science of Michael Crichton, Forensic Nurse Magazine, Nature Biotechnology, Information Systems for Biotechnology News Report, Law and Order Magazine, PharmaTechnology Magazine,* and educational testing publications. His books, *Sickle Cell Disease* (2008) and *The Genetic Code* (2011), were published by Chelsea House. He also wrote and teaches an online course in forensic science for writers through Ed2Go.com.